KATHARINE GRAHAM

KATHARINE GRAHAM

Sandy Asirvatham

CHELSEA HOUSE PUBLISHERS
PHILADELPHIA

Frontispiece: Katharine Graham worked for the *Washington Post* for more than five decades and served as its publisher for more than 15 years.

Chelsea House Publishers
EDITOR IN CHIEF Sally Cheney
DIRECTOR OF PRODUCTION Kim Shinners
PRODUCTION MANAGER Pamela Loos
ART DIRECTOR Sara Davis
EDITOR LeeAnne Gelletly
PRODUCTION EDITOR Diann Grasse
LAYOUT 21st Century Publishing and Communications, Inc.

The Chelsea House World Wide Web address is
http://www.chelseahouse.com

First Printing
1 3 5 7 9 8 6 4 2

Library of Congress Cataloging-in-Publication Data

Asirvatham, Sandy.
    Katharine Graham / Sandy Asirvatham.
        p.cm — (Women of achievement)
    Includes bibliographical references.
    Summary: The life of the woman who was publisher and later chair-person and CEO of the Washington Post Company, and who in 1997 received the Pulitzer Prize for biography.
    ISBN 0-7910-6310-0 (alk. paper)—ISBN 0-7910-6311-9 (pbk. : alk. paper)
    1. Graham, Katharine, 1917—Juvenile literature. 2. Publishers and publishing—United States—Biography—Juvenile literature.
    3. Washington post (Washington, D.C.: 1974)—History—Juvenile literature. 4. Newspaper publishing—Washington (D.C.)—History—20th century—Juvenile literature. [1. Graham, Katharine, 1917–
    2. Publishers and publishing. 3. Washington post (Washington, D.C.: 1974). 4. Women—Biography.] I. Title. II. Series.

Z473.G7 A84 2001
070.5'092—dc21
[B]   2001037254

CONTENTS

WOMEN of ACHIEVEMENT

Jane Addams
SOCIAL WORKER

Madeleine Albright
STATESWOMAN

Marian Anderson
SINGER

Susan B. Anthony
WOMAN SUFFRAGIST

Joan of Arc
FRENCH SAINT AND HEROINE

Clara Barton
AMERICAN RED CROSS FOUNDER

Rachel Carson
BIOLOGIST AND AUTHOR

Cher
SINGER AND ACTRESS

Cleopatra
QUEEN OF EGYPT

Hillary Rodham Clinton
FIRST LADY AND ATTORNEY

Katie Couric
JOURNALIST

Diana, Princess of Wales
HUMANITARIAN

Emily Dickinson
POET

Elizabeth Dole
POLITICIAN

Amelia Earhart
AVIATOR

Gloria Estefan
SINGER

Jodie Foster
ACTRESS AND DIRECTOR

Ruth Bader Ginsburg
SUPREME COURT JUSTICE

Katherine Graham
PUBLISHER

Helen Hayes
ACTRESS

Mahalia Jackson
GOSPEL SINGER

Helen Keller
HUMANITARIAN

**Ann Landers/
Abigail Van Buren**
COLUMNISTS

Barbara McClintock
BIOLOGIST

Margaret Mead
ANTHROPOLOGIST

Julia Morgan
ARCHITECT

Toni Morrison
AUTHOR

Grandma Moses
PAINTER

Lucretia Mott
WOMAN SUFFRAGIST

Sandra Day O'Connor
SUPREME COURT JUSTICE

Rosie O'Donnell
ENTERTAINER AND COMEDIAN

Georgia O'Keeffe
PAINTER

Eleanor Roosevelt
DIPLOMAT AND HUMANITARIAN

Wilma Rudolph
CHAMPION ATHLETE

Diane Sawyer
JOURNALIST

Elizabeth Cady Stanton
WOMAN SUFFRAGIST

Martha Stewart
ENTREPRENEUR

Harriet Beecher Stowe
AUTHOR AND ABOLITIONIST

Barbra Streisand
ENTERTAINER

Amy Tan
AUTHOR

Elizabeth Taylor
ACTRESS AND ACTIVIST

Mother Teresa
HUMANITARIAN AND
RELIGIOUS LEADER

Barbara Walters
JOURNALIST

Edith Wharton
AUTHOR

Phillis Wheatley
POET

Oprah Winfrey
ENTERTAINER

"REMEMBER THE LADIES"

MATINA S. HORNER

"Remember the Ladies." That is what Abigail Adams wrote to her husband John, then a delegate to the Continental Congress, as the Founding Fathers met in Philadelphia to form a new nation in March of 1776. "Be more generous and favorable to them than your ancestors. Do not put such unlimited power in the hands of the Husbands. If particular care and attention is not paid to the Ladies," Abigail Adams warned, "we are determined to foment a Rebellion, and will not hold ourselves bound by any Laws in which we have no voice, or Representation."

The words of Abigail Adams, one of the earliest American advocates of women's rights, were prophetic. Because when we have not "remembered the ladies," they have, by their words and deeds, reminded us so forcefully of the omission that we cannot fail to remember them. For the history of American women is as interesting and varied as the history of our nation as a whole. American women have played an integral part in founding, settling, and building our country. Some we remember as remarkable women who—against great odds—achieved distinction in the public arena: Anne Hutchinson, who in the 17th century became a charismatic religious leader; Phillis Wheatley, an 18th-century black slave who became a poet; Susan B. Anthony, whose name is synonymous with the 19th-century women's rights movement, and who led the struggle to enfranchise women; and in the 20th century, Amelia Earhart, the first woman to cross the Atlantic Ocean by air.

These extraordinary women certainly merit our admiration, but other women, "common women," many of them all but forgotten, should also be recognized for their contributions to American thought and culture. Women have been community builders; they have founded schools and formed voluntary associations to help those in need; they have assumed the major responsibility for rearing children, passing on from one generation to the next the values that keep a culture alive. These and innumerable other contributions, once ignored, are now being recognized by scholars, students, and the public. It is exciting and gratifying that a part of our history that was hardly acknowledged a few generations ago is now being studied and brought to light.

In recent decades, the field of women's history has grown from obscurity to a politically controversial splinter movement to academic respectability, in many cases mainstreamed into such traditional disciplines as history, economics, and psychology. Scholars of women, both female and male, have organized research centers at such prestigious institutions as Wellesley College, Stanford University, and the University of California. Other notable centers for women's studies are the Center for the American Woman and Politics at the Eagleton Institute of Politics at Rutgers University; the Henry A. Murray Research Center for the Study of Lives, at Radcliffe College; and the Women's Research and Education Institute, the research arm of the Congressional Caucus on Women's Issues. Other scholars and public figures have established archives and libraries, such as the Schlesinger Library on the History of Women in America, at Radcliffe College, and the Sophia Smith Collection, at Smith College, to collect and preserve the written and tangible legacies of women.

From the initial donation of the Women's Rights Collection in 1943, the Schlesinger Library grew to encompass vast collections documenting the manifold accomplishments of American women. Simultaneously, the women's movement in general and the academic discipline of women's studies in particular also began with a narrow definition and gradually expanded their mandate. Early causes, such as woman suffrage and social reform, abolition, and organized labor were joined by newer concerns, such as the history of women in business and the professions and in politics and government; the study of the family; and social issues such as health policy and education.

Women, as historian Arthur M. Schlesinger, jr., once pointed out, "have constituted the most spectacular casualty of traditional history. They have made up at least half the human race, but you could never tell that by looking at the books historians write." The new breed of historians is remedying that omission. They have written books about immigrant women and about working-class women who struggled for survival in cities and about black women who met the challenges of life in rural areas. They are telling the stories of women who, despite the barriers of tradition and economics, became lawyers and doctors and public figures.

The women's studies movement has also led scholars to question traditional interpretations of their respective disciplines. For example, the study of war has traditionally been an exercise in military and political analysis, an examination of strategies planned and executed by men. But scholars of women's history have pointed out that wars have also been periods of tremendous change and even opportunity for women, because the very absence of men on the home front enabled them to expand their educational, economic, and professional activities and to assume leadership in their homes.

The early scholars of women's history showed a unique brand of courage in choosing to investigate new subjects and take new approaches to old ones. Often, like their subjects, they endured criticism and even ostracism by their academic colleagues. But their efforts have unquestionably been worthwhile, because with the publication of each new study and book another piece of the historical patchwork is sewn into place, revealing an increasingly comprehensive picture of the role of women in our rich and varied history.

Such books on groups of women are essential, but books that focus on the lives of individuals are equally indispensable. Biographies can be inspirational, offering their readers the example of people with vision who have looked outside themselves for their goals and have often struggled against great obstacles to achieve them. Marian Anderson, for instance, had to overcome racial bigotry in order to perfect her art and perform as a concert singer. Isadora Duncan defied the rules of classical dance to find true artistic freedom. Jane Addams had to break down society's notions of the proper role for women in order to create new social situations, notably the settlement house. All of these women had to come to terms both with themselves and with the world in which they lived. Only then could they move ahead as pioneers in their chosen callings.

Biography can inspire not only by adulation but also by realism. It helps us to see not only the qualities in others that we hope to emulate, but also, perhaps, the weaknesses that made them "human." By helping us identify with the subject on a more personal level they help us feel that we, too, can achieve such goals. We read about Eleanor Roosevelt, for instance, who occupied a unique and seemingly enviable position as the wife of the president. Yet we can sympathize with her inner dilemma; an inherently shy woman, she had to force herself to live a most public life in order to use her position to benefit others. We may not be able to imagine ourselves having the immense poetic talent of Emily Dickinson, but from her story we can understand the challenges faced by a creative woman who was expected to fulfill many family responsibilities. And though few of us will ever reach the level of athletic accomplishment displayed by Wilma Rudolph or Babe Zaharias, we can still appreciate their spirit, their overwhelming will to excel.

A biography is a multifaceted lens. It is first of all a magnification, the intimate examination of one particular life. But at the same time, it is a wide-angle lens, informing us about the world in which the subject lived. We come away from reading about one life knowing more about the social, political, and economic fabric of the time. It is for this reason, perhaps, that the great New England essayist Ralph Waldo Emerson wrote in 1841, "There is properly no history: only biography." And it is also why biography, and particularly women's biography, will continue to fascinate writers and readers alike.

Graham poses with an edition of the Washington Post *in 1964. A year before, she became publisher of the paper, taking over the position of her deceased husband.*

1

LOSING PHIL, FINDING KAY

In the late summer of 1963, 44-year-old Katharine Graham allowed herself a moment of hope that the ordeal of the past months and years would soon be behind her. Katherine—nicknamed Kay—was the daughter of an immensely wealthy businessman named Eugene Meyer and had been married for 22 years to Phil Graham, publisher of the *Washington Post*, one of several competing local daily newspapers then available in the nation's capital. Kay and Phil had four children whom they raised in two residences: a city home in Washington, D.C., and a beautiful country farmhouse in rural Virginia.

Although she had been an intellectually and politically active college student and had spent her early twenties working as a newspaper reporter—one of the rare females to hold such a job at that time—Graham eventually accommodated herself to her generation's traditional role of wife, mother, social secretary, and general manager of the family. Her beloved husband, however, had turned out to need far more care than she could have ever imagined when she was a young and hopeful bride.

Phil Graham, Katharine's husband and publisher of the Post *until 1963, suffered from manic depression and eventually took his own life.*

Phil Graham had always been a charismatic, brilliant fellow, but in the past few years his behavior had grown erratic. After suffering a nervous breakdown, he was diagnosed with manic depression, a mental illness that causes individuals to cycle through intense, extreme mood swings—hyperactive manic phases alternating with deep, dark, suicidal depressions. Phil hit a real low point in the winter holiday season of 1962–63, when he announced to a shocked and bewildered Graham that he was having a love affair with a young woman he met at the office. After first pledging to break off the affair, Phil suddenly decided to divorce his wife. In the midst of this emotional crisis, Graham had to contend with the fact that her husband, who had been given control of the *Washington Post* by her father, Eugene Meyer, was now trying to take the newspaper—Graham's family legacy—away from her. A few months later, almost as dramatically as he left, Phil dropped the divorce suit and the bid for ownership of the *Post*, returned to Graham begging her forgiveness, and agreed to be admitted to a mental hospital called Chestnut Lodge.

Manic depression was only beginning to be categorized and understood, and even today there are ongoing debates regarding how best to treat it. In the 1960s there were generally two options offered for treatment—electric shock therapy or mind-altering drugs. Neither of these therapies were proven effective or completely safe. Phil resisted these treatments and instead relied upon the old-fashioned European "talking cure" of psychotherapy (first institutionalized by Sigmund Freud). In retrospect, Katharine would wonder how she could have ever trusted Phil's psychoanalyst, Dr. Leslie Farber—a man who believed that Phil's powerful inner demons could be exorcised simply by discussing philosophical questions and childhood memories.

One of the problems with manic depression is that the sufferer, in his or her manic phase, may talk and behave in ways that seem perfectly rational and balanced. Always articulate and charming, Phil managed to convince his doctors at Chestnut Lodge that he was feeling well enough to spend a weekend at the family's country retreat, the wooded, 350-acre estate known as Glen Welby, where Phil had taught his children to hunt, fish, and sail. Thirty-five years later, in her frank, insightful autobiography called *Personal History*,

Graham described how it all came about:

> There was a sharp difference of opinion among the doctors
> at the Lodge about whether [Phil's leaving the hospital]
> was a good idea, but no one ever asked me if there was
> liquor or sleeping pills at the farm, nor did I think to
> mention the guns we had there. I, who certainly knew the
> farm was stocked with guns that Phil used for sport, was
> completely deluded by his seeming progress, lack of
> visible depression, and determination to get well; in fact,
> I was optimistic about his ability to do so.

On August 3, 1963, a family chauffeur picked
Phil Graham up at the Lodge, and then came
around for Kay Graham at their house in northwest
Washington, D.C. They drove out to Glen Welby,
ate some lunch on the back porch, chatted, and
listened to classical records. Shortly after, Phil told
Graham he was going off to a spare bedroom to take
a nap. A few minutes later she heard the explosion
of a gun going off in the house. She bolted into the
bathroom and found her husband dead by his own
hand. The ordeal she thought was over had only just
begun. Graham described the horrible moment in
her memoir:

> It was so profoundly shocking and traumatizing—he
> was so obviously dead and the wounds were so ghastly
> to look at—that I just ran into the next room and buried
> my head in my hands, trying to absorb that this had
> really happened, this dreadful thing that had hung over
> us for the last six years, which he had discussed with
> me and with the doctors, but which he had not been
> talking about in recent weeks. . . . It had never occurred
> to me that he must have planned the whole day at Glen
> Welby to get to his guns as a way of freeing himself
> forever from the watchful eyes of the doctors—and
> the world.

Phil Graham left no suicide note. He was given a
huge, public funeral on August 6 at the Washington

National Cathedral, and was buried at Oak Hill,
right across the street from their Washington, D.C.,
home. His death was an intense shock to his children,
his friends, and the many people who respected and
admired him, from the humblest secretaries at the
Post to some of the most powerful politicians in
D.C., including President John F. Kennedy and
Vice President Lyndon B. Johnson. But most of all,
it was a shock to Kay Graham. She had done exactly
what the era demanded of her: she had become a
model wife, gradually but inevitably allowing her
identity to be overshadowed and consumed by her
husband's life—both the luminous heights of his
worldly ambitions and success, and the dark depths
of his mental illness. She was suddenly bereft of the
person who had controlled the structure and mean-
ing of her life.

Of course, she still had her beloved children:
Elizabeth (Lally), Donald (Donny), William (Bill),
and Stephen (Stevie). She was thinking almost
entirely of them and not of herself when she
decided, hesitantly and with much fear and anxiety,
to hang on to the family business by replacing Phil
as head of the *Post*. Money was not the issue—she
still had her inheritance and she also could have sold
the company and lived comfortably off the profit, as
many widows in her position would have done.
Shortly after the funeral, one of Graham's friends—
a man named Chip Bohlen who was then a lawyer at
the U.S. State Department—reflected the attitudes
of the day when he said to her, "You're not going to
work, are you? You mustn't—you are young and
attractive and you'll get remarried." Graham may
have harbored such thoughts herself, but the fact
remained that the *Post* was her father's legacy to his
children, and she felt it was her duty to preserve and
nurture the company for the new generation.

What Graham did not predict at the time was that

her sense of obligation to keep the paper in the family would turn out to be more like a calling—a destiny that she might have missed entirely had her husband recovered from his illness and stayed alive and active in the business. A complete novice at management, Graham threw herself into the business life of the *Post* and the other news organizations owned by the company. The early years were very rough, as she battled with her associates' inability to trust her and her own private insecurities in taking on the role as leader. By the late 1960s and early 1970s, through a combination of hard work and luck, Graham would lead the transformation of the *Washington Post* into the most powerful newspaper in the most powerful city in the world. She would eventually steer the company through some of its finest hours—as well as some of its darkest moments. Along the way, she would make a million mistakes and try her best to learn from them. And in the process, she would evolve from a shy, insecure, second-class citizen in her own marriage as Mrs. Philip L. Graham into a bold and confident leader as Katharine Graham, publisher of the *Washington Post* and president and chair of the Washington Post Company.

Three decades earlier, her father had shown some glimmer of belief that a smart young girl like his Kay could one day grow up to play an important role in the publishing empire he worked to build. He encouraged her to study hard, write well, offer her opinions tenaciously, and pursue her goals ambitiously. He sent her to receive a fine, challenging education at Vassar College and the University of Chicago and helped her get her first newspaper job as a labor reporter for the *San Francisco News*. He spoke occasionally of her grand future at the *Post*, but then he succumbed to the traditions of the times. When Graham was married, Eugene

Meyer sold the controlling portion of stock shares to his new son-in-law and put him in charge of the company, not his daughter. He had always loved and supported her, but ultimately he just could not envision a woman in charge of a newspaper, nor could most men and women of the era, including Graham herself—not yet.

Vice president Al Gore (left) and others present to Graham the 1997 Four Freedoms Award, given to an American whose career reflects democratic ideals.

A young Katharine sits with her father, Eugene Meyer, in their home in Washington, D.C. The Washington Post *has been a family-run business ever since Meyer bought the newspaper in 1933.*

2

A PROPER
YOUNG LADY

Katharine Graham's parents were both highly unusual people in many ways. Eugene Meyer, born in 1875 in Los Angeles, hailed from an old Jewish family with roots in the Alsace-Lorraine region of France. Eugene's father was strict and not very loving, while his mother suffered from depression and poor physical health: she had been broken mentally and physically by the stress of giving birth to eight children before the age of 32 under the crude medical conditions of the era. By the time Eugene was in his thirties, he had escaped the material discomforts of his youth by turning a $600 investment in the stock market into many millions of dollars; but he would always remain a somewhat distant and detached person, the legacy of his cold and loveless upbringing.

Eugene's hard work, intelligence, and judicious nature would serve him well in various endeavors over the decades. Early on, he pioneered a new philosophy of stock investment that relied on in-depth research of companies. Today this practice is routine on Wall Street, but back then it was a novelty.

Agnes Ernst had in some ways quite a different background. A childhood resident of Pelham Heights, New York, she came from a long line of Lutheran ministers with origins in northern Germany. But Agnes shared with Eugene similar emotional and material deprivations during her upbringing. She was also raised in an austere, puritanical manner, although her father did not live up to the standards Agnes would enforce on her daughter Katharine. He was a fairly successful lawyer, but he drank, womanized, and neglected to pay bills. He tried his hand at writing plays and books, but failed miserably.

Agnes had loved her father when she was young and he was still relatively sober and stable, but she harbored a terrible resentment of his selfish and reckless ways. In her late teens, she took it upon herself to become independent, and won a scholarship to Barnard College. In those days, respectable college girls were generally groomed to become teachers or secretaries, so when Agnes told her parents that she planned to become a newspaper reporter, her mother wept and her father said, "I would rather see you dead."

Agnes stuck to her guns, though, and by the time she met her future husband in 1908, she was already established as a freelance art critic for the *New York Sun*. An exceptional beauty, Agnes was courted by many suitors, which only made worse her childhood tendency to be vain and self-centered. In her autobiography, *Personal History*, Katherine Graham sadly admitted that she was not sure if her mother actually loved her father when she agreed to marry him. For one thing, Agnes shared the latent anti-Semitism that prevailed among much of the population during the era. She may also have been attracted to his money and prospects more than to the man himself. Whatever the truth of her emotions, Agnes did marry Eugene in 1909 and moved to his farmhouse in Mount Kisco, New York. Eugene generously paid off Agnes's father's considerable debts and supported the broken old man until he died in 1913.

Katharine was very active during her childhood, playing several sports, taking piano lessons, and performing in school plays. Here she poses on the deck of a ship.

In those days—decades before the women's movement—an independent, proto-feminist woman like Agnes had a lot of trouble adjusting to married life, as she later recalled in her memoir: "So many of my married college friends had renounced their intellectual interests and lost themselves in a routine of diapers, dinners, and smug contentment with life, that I was determined this should not happen to me. I wanted a big family, but I also wanted to continue my life as an individual."

According to her daughter, Agnes Meyer never really achieved a healthy balance in this regard. She gave birth to four children in quick succession—Florence, Elizabeth, William, and then Katharine, born on June 16, 1917. Agnes then essentially handed them over to be raised by a nursemaid and a governess. More than half a century later, Katharine retained very fond memories of her caretakers, but remembers her mother being an extremely self-centered and self-absorbed person—conscientious in her parenting, but not very loving.

As complex and contradictory as Katharine's relationship with her mother was, she still felt closer to her than to her father, who was often awkward with his children and continued to have trouble expressing his emotions even when they grew to be adults. In general, the Meyer household let many important issues pass in silence, and certain topics were considered completely taboo—for example, money, sex, and Eugene's Jewish heritage. Yet in the end, Kay recalled, her father "somehow conveyed his belief in me without ever articulating it, and that was the single most sustaining thing in my life. That was what saved me."

In 1933, Eugene Meyer heard that one of the newspapers in Washington, D.C., the *Post*, was about to go bankrupt. Five years earlier, Meyer had offered $5 million to purchase the company, but the owners were not willing to sell. During this period, Meyer was working in various government jobs under the administration of President Herbert Hoover. Much of his work in public service involved trying to dig the country out of the Great Depression, the economic disaster that had left hundreds of thousands of working-class Americans in a desperate state of unemployment and poverty. Meyer's efforts resulted in some effective relief legislation, but his overall ambition to restore the nation's economic health was ultimately more than one man could handle. A staunch Republican, Meyer decided to leave public office in 1932, when the country elected a Democratic president, Franklin D. Roosevelt. So the news about the *Post* came at a perfect time. Meyer purchased the deeply troubled news organization at the rock-bottom price of $825,000.

The *Post*, the number five paper in D.C., was in dismal shape both financially and editorially when Meyer bought it. He had dreams of turning it into

a profitable and high quality news organ that would report objectively, fairly, and thoroughly on political matters and would, very importantly, remain far above the political influences. In the beginning he had a naive faith that his previous successes in business and government would adequately prepare him for the world of journalism.

In 1933, the Post, *like many newspapers during the Great Depression, faced bankruptcy. It was sold to Eugene Meyer during an auction held at the steps of its office.*

At the time, Katharine was in her junior year at a private girls' high school called Madeira, where she was preparing to take her college boards. As the Meyer household was one of little communication, no one bothered to tell Kay about her father's newspaper purchase—an event she learned about only when she went home that summer.

Kay Meyer was a girl of her times—her priorities were trying to fit in with other girls, and learning how to interact with boys. She was tall for her age, naturally shy, and a bit awkward, though she later recalled how she found popularity: "When I was about seventeen, I made a determined effort to learn how to appeal to the boys in the stag line at parties and dances. I noticed that if you laughed uproariously at the silliest joke and acted lively, as though you were having a wonderful time, the boys thought you were attractive and appealing."

But Katharine was also beginning to develop her own personal interests. She played varsity basketball, hockey, and track. She also sang in the chorus, played piano, appeared in school plays, and, most notably for her career later on, wrote for the school magazine, the *Tatler*. Although she thought of herself as a shy and awkward person, much like her father, Kay apparently struck other people as a confident and determined young woman. According to a prophecy in her senior yearbook, Kay Meyer was destined to become "a Big Shot in the newspaper racket."

A strong personality and potential leader in some ways, the young woman who would become Katharine Graham was still essentially a follower and conformist, even on apparently important decisions in life. In 1934, she entered Vassar, an all-female college she chose only because her beloved older sister Elizabeth (Bis) had gone there and because most of her fellow high school seniors would also be enrolling there. Ironically, however, her arrival at the college set the stage for her first attempts at becoming truly independent.

Bis and Kay's brother, Bill, were living and studying in London, while Kay's oldest sister, Flo, had entered the working world as a professional ballroom dancer. Young Ruthie was still in high school. Katharine was on her own trying to navigate the perils and confusions of late adolescence and young adulthood. She recalled, "While my older sisters and brother were thus venturing into the real world, I was so unworldly

An avid student, Kay Meyer (front row, second from right) discovered her passion for writing while reporting for the school newspaper at Madeira, a private girls' school, from which she graduated in 1934.

that it was difficult for me to function. My new circle of friends and range of activities all looked appropriate and right, but I found them confusing and felt lost. I had a particularly hard time concentrating on my work and reading."

College is ideally a place where a young person may be able to learn the ropes quickly by watching his or her peers closely. Even at an elite school like Vassar, Kay Meyer stood out because of her extraordinary wealth and pampered upbringing. She had never shopped for clothes herself, and in high school her entire wardrobe consisted only of elegant custom-made dresses chosen by her mother. Just before arriving at Vassar, Kay did manage to buy herself some skirts and sweaters. She recalled how she wore one yellow cardigan through the first weeks of school until Thanksgiving, and then somebody suggested she should wash it. She had seen other girls' newly hand-washed sweaters stretched out on towels in the bathroom, but hadn't figured out that she was supposed to be doing the same. At home, she had always simply discarded her dirty laundry without a second thought, and (thanks to multitudes of servants) it would show up cleaned and pressed in her drawers a day or two later. She recalled that she eventually sent the yellow sweater out to a cleaner, and never learned how to wash one.

Although it took a long time for Katharine to shed her ignorance of such practical matters—cooking, cleaning, decorating her dorm room, buying clothes, keeping to a budget, or understanding the appropriate price of things—she was quickly beginning to absorb an understanding of larger political issues. Back at home, Eugene and Agnes Meyer were both fiercely and vocally opposed to President Roosevelt's "New Deal"—a broad attempt to provide services and financial support to needy Americans, which became the root of today's welfare, unemployment, social security, and other social "safety net" programs.

At Vassar Kay heard pro-Roosevelt, pro-New Deal arguments for the first time from some of her professors and colleagues and eventually found herself agreeing with them.

During her freshman and sophomore years, Katharine was often disorganized and undisciplined as a student, although in some ways she made up for her shortcomings with her genuine intellectual enthusiasm. She got into heated arguments with her history teacher, fell in love with the fiction of the great German writer Thomas Mann, and became involved in student political organizations. In the summers, she went home to Mount Kisco and started writing for a local newspaper. Her first article with her byline, or name, on it was a piece about women doctors, a novelty in those days.

Although Kay was beginning to follow in her mother's footsteps in becoming a writer, she would later recall that she never received praise from her mother in that pursuit. Agnes Meyer was still a working journalist, who sometimes fed her ego by telling her daughter how she had already read, critiqued, and even memorized the books that were Kay's college assignments. Still, Agnes's career both inspired and intimidated her daughter.

While her lifelong struggles with her mother continued, Kay began growing closer to her father during her college years. He was respectful of her political opinions and personal decisions even when he disagreed with them. He could coolly discuss her connections with radical left-wing activists, her participation in student union activities, and other aspects of her college experience. After Katharine's sophomore year at Vassar, Eugene Meyer allowed her to transfer to the University of Chicago, an urban, coeducational, and intellectually charged atmosphere that could not have been more different from the polite ladies' finishing-school setting of Vassar.

In Chicago, Kay fell in with a group of male and female friends who loved to talk about politics, books, and ideas and who spent hours at the local college beer parlor arguing, singing songs, and simply enjoying one another's conversation. Under the teachings of Mortimer Adler and other famous professors, Katharine developed into a committed liberal—against the developing European fascism in Italy and Germany, but sympathetic toward the quasi-socialist ideas of the growing U.S. labor movement.

In her personal and social life, however, she was still a very conservative person. Even as the world was changing so rapidly politically, so near the beginning of the Second World War, Katharine adhered to traditional guidelines of what was expected from a young woman in her manners and speech. She was, after all, a proper young lady, as well as a daughter of wealth, privilege, and power. She was also the daughter of a mother who demanded social perfection from her children. Although her parents were glad to provide her with an excellent higher education and her father sometimes hinted at the idea that she would one day help him run his newspaper business, the underlying assumption was always that she would first and foremost become a wife and mother.

Despite such unspoken but implied strictures, Kay had a brief chance to loosen up and live the life of an independent young career woman in her years after graduating from the University of Chicago in June 1938. She moved for several months to San Francisco, where her father had helped arrange a job for her as a reporter on a small newspaper called the *San Francisco News*. Katharine was bewildered at first by the demands of the job, but within a few weeks she began to feel comfortable, even ambitious. She became the legman, or helper, to the paper's primary reporter on labor matters. She

quickly grew familiar with her beat, spending late nights in bars getting to know union leaders and organizers. She conducted very creditable reporting during a conflict among longshoremen (dockworkers) and the big distribution companies that depended on these laborers. Her editors praised her work and her coworkers regarded her as an intelligent, charming addition to the company. A jovial office picture taken at the time shows Kay seated at a desk near her typewriter, dressed in a tweed suit and smart hat, pretending to give orders to three men—also reporters, presumably—who stand tall and salute the young lady.

In 1948, Katherine graduated from the University of Chicago and moved to San Francisco, where she got her first journalism experience as a labor reporter.

After her apprenticeship in San Francisco, Katharine returned to Washington, D.C., at her father's request, and joined the staff of the *Post* as an editorial page employee. There she did no firsthand reporting, but helped write and edit official opinion pieces on current events. It was a politically exciting yet anxious time for Kay, as for most of the paper's reporters and writers. Hitler's long-threatened territorial invasions had finally come to pass, spreading war across Europe. As a rookie reporter, Katharine did not write on world politics. However, she did get a chance to produce light editorials on less weighty issues. In her autobiography she offered the titles of some of her articles from her early career in news: "On Being a Horse," "Brains and Beauty," "Mixed Drinks," "Lou Gehrig," and "Spotted Fever."

As Katharine matured into a young woman, her mother Agnes Meyer was growing more and more emotionally unstable. Kay recalled one occasion in particular that demonstrated her mother's declining mental health. The incident took place in the summer of 1937 when the whole family was out riding horses at the Graham ranch in Wyoming. For some reason, Agnes's horse suddenly broke from the pack and ran away. Katherine's younger sister Ruthie, an excellent rider, took off in pursuit along with some of the cowboys who were riding with the family. After the horse was caught and somehow stopped, Agnes went completely to pieces, fought with her husband, and fled from him into her cabin, where she began drinking. The family was deeply disturbed.

When her father could no longer handle her mother's outbursts, it usually fell upon Kay to try to calm her mother down. She grew to like the responsibility in some ways, although she also resented how much of the family's time and energy was used up by her mother's problems.

Agnes Meyer, Katharine's mother, was a famous speaker on several social issues and a source of inspiration for her daughter. Like Phil Graham, Meyer also had her share of emotional problems.

In psychological circles, it is often observed that children of mentally ill, abusive, or alcoholic parents will eventually be drawn to partners or spouses who harbor many of the same traits—even if those traits aren't obvious at first. Perhaps this dynamic was secretly at work when Kay met Philip Graham, her future husband.

Their first encounter was like something out of an

old Hollywood farce. Some of Kay's reporter friends from the *Post* lived in a so-called "bachelor house"—similar to the "group houses" for young unmarried people that still dominate certain neighborhoods in D.C., except these were always strictly single-sex, most often for men. While Kay was in one of these houses with her buddies John Oakes and Hedley Donovan, she leaned at the window to call out to another group of friends and acquaintances she saw on the sidewalk. As she did so, the window screen fell out, and landed right onto the heads of these people—including one man she hadn't met yet, Philip Graham.

As Kay soon learned, Graham was a brilliant young graduate of Harvard Law School who was then clerking for a Supreme Court judge. He was reputed in their social circle as handsome, gifted, articulate, and exceptionally witty. Within a few months of the window screen incident—after he had ended his engagement to one woman, proposed to a second woman, and then broken off that second engagement, as well—Phil started courting Kay very fervently and insistently, as young men of the era were apt to do. After a very short time, he declared his intentions: "He told me that he loved me and said we would be married and go to Florida, if I could live with only two dresses, because I had to understand that he would never take anything from my father or be involved with him and we would live on what he made." The intensity and the manful pride of his words took Kay's breath away. She admitted to feeling somewhat startled.

Kay hesitated at first, but she couldn't help but be charmed and dazzled. In retrospect, perhaps she could have interpreted Phil's impulsive and resolute proposal as a sign of his essentially unwell psyche—as a symptom of his "manic" side. But at the time, all she could do was be excited that this charismatic, fascinating man was madly in love with her, and she with him. Detailing their courtship, Katharine related, "For the first time I had found a man who was the right mix of intellectual, physical and social charm, and warm and funny on top of that."

In this picture taken in the early years of her marriage, Katharine Graham plays a new phonograph model of a radio. Kay, who had a privileged childhood with few household duties, had some trouble adjusting to the duties of domestic life after marrying Phil.

3

MRS. PHILIP L. GRAHAM

Phil Graham and Eugene Meyer argued about politics the first time they met—an argument so vehement that Kay was worried her father would not approve of her future husband. Eugene later admitted that he had had a wonderful time with the young man and "liked him fine," according to Katharine's recollection of the event. Agnes Meyer was also impressed by Phil, first by his masculine jaw line and easygoing demeanor, and later by what she perceived to be his great intelligence and strength. The young couple married at the Meyer house in Mount Kisco on June 5, 1940, among a small group of family and close friends. The famous photographer Edward Steichen just happened to be among the guests, and he took photographs that Katharine would cherish for the rest of her life. She detailed the special day in her autobiography: "My dress was designed by me and made to order at Bergdorf Goodman. It was long, as I had wanted, and austerely simple but beautiful, made of heavy eggshell silk, with a scarf edged with my grandmother's lace. I carried orchids and wore orange blossoms in my hair but no veil."

After a few days at the Carlyle House in New York City, the newlyweds took a steamship to Bermuda where they bicycled, played tennis, swam, and tried not to worry about world events, such as Germany's aggressive campaigns in Europe (France was just about to fall to Germany in the war). Shortly after returning from their honeymoon, Phil and Kay embarked on another very important trip, their first together to Phil's hometown in Florida. They made the journey via a Buick convertible Katharine had inherited from her brother. She admitted to feeling ill at ease during her first visit to Phil's family, partially because she had never met them and had never visited the South, having lived in the cities of Washington, Chicago, and San Francisco and the countryside of Mount Kisco.

Phil Graham had grown up on a farm near the Everglades, in a family that had seen both good times and bad times, financially speaking. They were generally smart, well-read, and industrious. His mother, Florence, who went by the nickname "Floss," was an admired, beloved woman who died of cancer when Phil was only 19. She and her husband, a shy and hardworking engineer, farmer, and businessman named Ernest (Ernie) Graham, had loved each other but quarreled frequently during their marriage. "His father had once, he told me, thrown a lamp at his mother in the course of a battle," Katharine remembered in her autobiography. "In one of the first quarrels [Phil and I] ever had, during which I slammed a door, he said he couldn't deal with that kind of scene, because of ones he had witnessed as a child, and pleaded that we never fight like that, so I didn't. This wasn't a good idea and led to many unresolved issues . . . an unhealthy situation in which things that upset one or the other of us didn't get aired."

In Florida, Kay met Ernie Graham, his second wife, Hilda, and their son Bob (Phil's half-brother, who many years later would become the governor of

Florida), as well as Phil's siblings Mary and Bill. It wasn't an easy trip for Katharine, who felt a little awkward among her new in-laws, although they were generally warm and welcoming. She also felt out of place among Phil's local college friends, Southern businessmen—"good ol' boys"—who were quite different from the urban, sophisticated Northeasterners she was accustomed to.

Back on her home turf, Kay had an easier time adjusting to married life. In a D.C. neighborhood near Georgetown, the couple rented a little house for $80 a month. Phil insisted from the start that they were going to live on their own salaries, not on the Meyer fortune, and was opposed to the idea of Kay becoming a stay-at-home wife.

Katharine, unaccustomed to knowing what things cost or how to handle even simple domestic duties such as ironing a dress, depended on her maid, Mattie, but also tried to learn some of the necessary household arts. She started keeping a small accounts book to track all their expenses—gas for the car, groceries, and personal items—although this earnest attempt at a little budgetary discipline did not last more than a few months. Phil was working hard for Supreme Court Justice Felix Frankfurter, a man who became his close friend and lifelong mentor. Meanwhile, Katharine was still at the *Post*, writing features for the "Brains" section of the Sunday paper (later called "Outlook"). She joined the Women's National Press Club, having received a recommendation from the *Post* managing editor, Casey Jones, who assessed her as a "thoroughly competent reporter."

Despite their long hours at their jobs, Phil and Kay grew close in this period and enjoyed married life. Decades later, Kay Graham would acknowledge that during that time, Phil really helped her separate herself from her family, liberating her from the myths and expectations surrounding what it meant to be a child of the great Eugene and Agnes Meyer. Phil taught Kay to take herself less seriously, to laugh at life and have fun.

However, even during this peaceful period, there were already subtle signs of the trouble that would lie ahead. Phil was a strong, decisive person, but it was often up to Kay to actually enact her husband's decisions. Within their marriage, Phil played the role of the manager, while Katharine was the laborer. "It wasn't until years later that I looked at the downside of all this and realized that, perversely, I had seemed to enjoy the role of doormat wife," Kay noted in her autobiography. "For whatever reason, I liked to be dominated and to be the implementer. But although I was thoroughly fascinated and charmed by Phil, I was also slightly resentful, when I thought about it, at feeling such complete dependence on another person."

In late 1941, the Japanese attacked a U.S. military base on Pearl Harbor, Hawaii—and after years of standing by nervously as Hitler engulfed Europe and the Japanese likewise sought to dominate large parts of the East—America was finally compelled to join the Second World War. Phil enlisted and was eventually trained as an intelligence officer in the U.S. Army. Meanwhile, Katharine was struggling to become a mother. Her first pregnancy ended in miscarriage. She carried her second pregnancy to full term, but during the delivery, her baby boy became tangled in his own umbilical cord and strangled to death. Kay was devastated by this loss, but eventually became pregnant again and gave birth to her daughter, Elizabeth, nicknamed Lally, on July 3, 1943.

Since she did not know the first thing about babies, Katharine hired a Scottish nurse who did most of the work of caring for the infant. At the time of Lally's birth, Phil had just been accepted as an officer at the Air Intelligence School in Harrisburg, Pennsylvania, so the newly expanded family was compelled to pack up and move there. Kay

Katharine suffered through a miscarriage and a failed delivery before giving birth to her daughter, Lally (center), in 1943. She later gave birth to Donald (right) and William (left). Steven would be born in 1951.

expressed her feelings regarding that moving day:

> The day we actually moved, Phil was recovering from a farewell party we'd hosted, so I packed up everything—the last object being an inert Phil—and got us to the new apartment. I didn't think much about it at the time, but this was the beginning of a pattern that I can now see was quite unhealthy: I was expected to perform all the pulling and hauling; Phil gave directions and put the fun in my life and the children's. Gradually I became the drudge and, what's more, accepted my role as a kind of second-class citizen. I think this definition of roles deepened as time went on and I became increasingly unsure of myself.

At this time, Phil's drinking was beginning to get a

bit excessive, and he also seemed to be ill quite often with the flu and other ailments. Although she did not see it clearly at the time, Katharine actually had a stronger drive than her husband, but continued to think of herself as the subordinate partner in their marriage. Soon after he completed his training in Harrisburg and the family moved back to Washington, Phil was assigned to a tour of duty in the Pacific. He would spend most of the rest of the war in the Philippines as an intelligence officer under George Kenney, General MacArthur's main air commander in the Pacific.

With Phil thousands of miles away engaged in the heat of the war effort, Kay stuck close to the new home they had recently purchased at 33rd and O Street in Georgetown and accustomed herself to the traditional roles of mother and manager of a household. On April 12, 1945—10 days after the sudden death of President Franklin Delano Roosevelt and the succession of Vice President Harry Truman to the nation's top job—Kay Graham gave birth to her son Donald. In September, Phil received his discharge from the armed forces, and was able to come home to meet their son for the first time.

After the war, although the future was as uncertain for the Grahams as it was for the rest of the country, it soon seemed clear that Phil's destiny in life was to be a public figure to wield power and influence. His wife's destiny, in contrast, seemed to be heading in the opposite direction, as she became consumed with the private domestic duties of maintaining a household, raising children, and entertaining guests. This division of labor was, at the time, a traditional one in almost all marriages in the United States. The American women's liberation movement would not gain momentum until the early 1970s, which would bring with it an influx of women in responsible positions in business, government, academia, science, and medicine.

Phil briefly considered his father's invitation to come

back to Florida and run the family dairy farm, but instead followed in his father-in-law's footsteps in the news media, taking a job as associate publisher of the *Post*. Eugene Meyer, who had been grooming his son-in-law to take over the newspaper company when he retired, was very pleased. In short order, Phil became one of the paper's best ad salesmen, making use of his law school-honed writing skills and general persuasiveness to convince company executives around the country to spend their advertising dollars in the *Post*.

This effort meant long, hard hours for Phil. Kay was left to take nearly complete charge of their domestic and social lives. Parental duties were in those days generally not shared between husband and wife, even in the smallest matters.

Although Katharine embraced her responsibilities as housewife and mother with love and enthusiasm, she struggled to learn how to thrive in her new domestic life. As a wealthy woman, she was able to hire a lot of help, of course: a nursemaid for the children, a cook, and a laundress. She recalled in her memoir that, nevertheless, "every day seemed hectic, and [the nurse's] days off sent me into a tailspin, in which I seemed more than ever all thumbs. One week when she was away, Donny fell out of his crib because I had left the side down, and out of his swing while I was weeding the yard. He ended up looking like Donald Duck, with his swollen upper lip sticking out an inch." Despite these occasional and perfectly typical calamities, Kay was learning how to run her house and to be an effective parent. She also had to learn how to cope with being married to a man whose work responsibilities had quickly accelerated, turning him into an overworked, fatigued companion and father to their children.

In June 1946, President Harry Truman called Eugene Meyer, offering him the position as president of the World Bank. Meyer was ready to move on to the next phase of his already highly accomplished life, so

Eugene Meyer leaves the White House after a meeting with President Truman in 1947. A year earlier, Meyer retired as publisher of the Post *and passed the paper on to Phil Graham, then just 31 years old.*

he passed the top job at the *Post* on to his 31-year-old son-in-law, who became the youngest publisher of a major newspaper in the United States. It was not going to be an easy job, since the *Post* had a great deal of competition from strong papers such as the *Washington Star* and the *Times-Herald*.

Katharine knew the state of the paper and sensed that the new position would be extremely difficult for anyone to fill. In her autobiography she admitted her fears regarding Phil's new role: "Although our friends and the press seemed to view Phil's rise to publisher positively, we knew things would not be easy. . . . Indeed, the paper itself was still struggling for its life. It had made profits in most of the war years, but was sliding right back to losses. The *Post* was certainly a marginal paper, and it felt like that to us."

The *Post* had it strengths, though, especially in its editorial staff, whose ranks included the influential columnist Walter Lippman and the controversial, highly original political cartoonist Herbert Block ("Herblock"). Although he was still new to the business, Phil navigated the *Post* through some small triumphs and put into place a few shrewd long-term strategies. He hired a new managing editor, Russ Wiggins, and helped develop the paper's first truly national staff. He searched for ways to improve the paper's basic news-reporting functions and introduced automation into the paper's general operations, beginning with the installation of IBM accounting machines as early as 1946. Phil also did his part to ensure the future success of the paper when he hired Ben Bradlee, an ace reporter who would eventually become the managing editor and much later guide his investigative reporting staff through some of its finest journalistic accomplishments.

Phil accomplished a great deal, although years later, Katharine Graham would question the wisdom of some of her husband's choices. Phil "often involved the *Post* in righting wrongs, as he saw them," she would recall in her autobiography. In 1949, for example, a huge riot began in Washington, D.C., when members of the leftist Progressive Party led a group of black children to a segregated white public swimming pool. As an opponent of segregation, Phil threatened to publish a front-page article about the riots if government officials did not make a move to desegregate the pools. To avoid the bad publicity, the powers-that-be capitulated to Phil's demands, closing the pools that summer and reopening them the next on an integrated basis. Katharine later wrote:

> This was a typical example of the way Phil used power, in this case the paper's, to accomplish something good. It worked, but at the same time it hurt the paper. It isn't—and probably wasn't even then—the way to run a newspaper. To keep a story out of the paper to achieve a purpose, even a fine one, is neither appropriate nor in the spirit of my father's definition of the duty of a newspaper: "To try to tell the truth. To find it out and tell it. To have a competent editorial department to interpret that truth."

However, this kind of criticism came much later, long after Katharine herself was forced to take on her late husband's job. When Phil headed the *Post,* she remained Phil's all-supportive helpmate as he worked to expand the business. In 1950 he bought a Florida television station and made several unsuccessful attempts to purchase the paper's main competitor, the *Times-Herald.*

Phil was also burdened with having to defend the *Post* against its political enemies on both the right (conservative) and left (liberal) ends of the spectrum. The Soviet Union was growing in power, and more and more citizens of Western nations perceived the expansion of communism as a major threat to their freedom and democracy. In this tense and anxious atmosphere, the ultraconservative demagogue Senator Joseph McCarthy came to power as head of the House Committee on Un-American Activities (HUAC), which began ferreting out suspected Soviet spies among American politicians, businessmen, filmmakers, writers, and others. HUAC operated largely on rumor and innuendo and imprisoned many people, ruining lives based on often very scanty evidence. Proof of actual spying was not necessary; merely having been a member of the Communist Party during college, for

example, was enough to tar someone's reputation. The *Post's* position was generally anticommunist, but its editorial page writers often took issue with HUAC's questionable tactics and methods, specifically its reliance on outrageous, unsubstantiated accusations against law-abiding citizens and the "witch-hunt" backdrop of its proceedings. Cartoonist Herblock eventually coined the term "McCarthyism" as a label for these questionable tactics and methods.

Phil Graham delivers a speech at a 1947 meeting hosted by the Herald Tribune. *Although he had no previous experience as a newspaper publisher, he accomplished much during his time with the* Post.

As a result of the *Post*'s critical stance, the paper was attacked for being liberal and even communist, which added to its financial problems and negative reputation. As if being considered a bane of the rabidly anti-communist right wing was not enough, the *Post* was also criticized by those on the left who believed the newspaper was not speaking out strongly enough against HUAC's infringement of civil liberties.

As the wife of a major newspaper publisher in the nation's capital, Kay Graham was one of the first to know about important U.S. political developments as they occurred, but she was not directly involved. As her world shrank to fit the demands of a busy housewife, Kay found herself growing increasingly dependent on Phil for her sense of self-worth. This became an especially tricky proposition as the Graham family grew in number—with the birth of William in 1948 and Stephen in 1951—and as Phil's responsibilities at work took him away from home for longer and longer periods. Katharine would eventually find her personality and her strength starting to crumble a bit under the intense, nearly claustrophobic pressure of a life spent solely attending to the needs of others. Her case of "caretaker syndrome" would only grow worse as Phil's physical and mental health deteriorated.

Paradoxically, at this time, Katharine's mother, Agnes Meyer, was living an exhilarating public life herself as a reporter and speaker on various political and social topics. Yet like so many ambitious and independent women of her generation, Agnes still implied to her daughters that the only truly important obligations in a woman's life are those to her husband and children. Kay thought this message was especially ironic coming from her mother, who, she felt, was a rather narcissistic and self-obsessed woman.

Kay had grown up in both a familial and overall cultural atmosphere in which a woman always stood

behind her man. She was neither insulted nor upset when her father decided to pass primary ownership of the Washington Post Company on to Phil, rather than her. Over the course of several months, Eugene and Agnes Meyer transferred 3,325 shares of the company to Phil Graham and another 1,325 shares to Kay, giving the couple a total of 5,000. Katharine recounted the transaction in her autobiography: "Phil received the larger share of the stock because, as Dad explained to me, no man should be in the position of working for his wife. Curiously I not only concurred but was in complete accord with this idea."

Katharine (second from left) and Phil (center) hold a meeting with Post *editors.*

Phil Graham testifies before the Senate on the need for revised election laws. Phil was well regarded as a public figure; only a few people knew about his severe mental problems.

4

MISSING THE WARNING SIGNS

Shortly after Katharine Graham published her poignant, revealing autobiography in 1997 (and received the coveted Pulitzer Prize for it), she confessed that she had considered omitting any discussion of her late husband's mental illness from the book. In an interview, Graham admitted that she began the project very naively. "I thought if you wrote an autobiography, that it had to tell your story," she confessed. "I just told my story." Reviewing the manuscript, Katharine and her children wondered whether the passages about their father's manic depression ought to be toned down or cut entirely. But Graham's editor said to her, "Look, if you don't print it all, he looks like an unpleasant drunk." So she decided to go ahead and tell the truth about Phil and his illness as fully as she could.

Fifty years earlier, Kay didn't even have a name for what was happening to her beloved husband. For a while, she explained, she assumed that it was mostly just a drinking problem. She never suspected that Phil was either ill or depressed.

The flip side of Phil's rage was his enormous energy, both for his responsibilities as a publisher and as head of his family. Indeed, in domestic matters, he was still operating as the "idea man" while Katharine did most of the actual work. For example, it was Phil's idea to purchase a country house in Virginia for summers and weekends, but it was Kay who actually went out and did the work to make it materialize. She explained that her husband's sense of humor and charm was always prevalent, however: "Phil was the fizz in our lives. He was the fun at the dinner table and in our country life. He had the ideas, the jokes, the games. . . . His ideas dominated our lives." At the time, Katharine was so in love with her witty, brilliant, exciting husband, she didn't notice he was frequently being critical and cutting in his remarks about her.

In later years, she admitted she would never quite figure out which aspects of Phil's personality were caused by his terrible affliction, and which were his "true" characteristics. (Undoubtedly, this is a common experience for those who live close to people suffering from manic depression, which was not well understood but is estimated to affect about 1 percent of the population.) Furthermore, she never connected her own growing lack of self-confidence with Phil's behavior toward her.

Under Phil's energetic guidance, the *Post* was beginning to thrive. In 1954, Phil was finally able to purchase the *Times-Herald*, the same rival newspaper for which Eugene Meyer had made an unsuccessful bid years earlier. The two papers merged, and the *Post* took over the former distribution and circulation of the *Times-Herald*. The combined papers now accounted for 70 percent of all household morning-newspaper readership in the Washington area. A few years later, the company purchased the magazine *Newsweek*, a fairly weak and insubstantial publication that would in time earn greater respect among a wider readership. Phil continued to play a major role in improving the editorial content of these publications by hiring excellent reporters and writers.

Meanwhile, his ongoing interest in political affairs kept him busy as well. Although the newspaper tried to remain politically neutral, as Eugene Meyer intended, Phil himself played a pivotal role in several important developments, such as the passage of the Civil Rights Act of 1957—which guaranteed voting rights to black Americans—and John F. Kennedy's decision to choose Lyndon B. Johnson as his running mate in his 1960 presidential campaign. Phil immersed himself in progressive political ideas and events, such as America's obligation to help less-developed countries (a topic that very few people discussed at the time). He gave persuasive speeches regarding the responsibility of those in power, including the press, to work for good causes, and help to right wrongs by addressing systematic injustices to the disenfranchised, or politically powerless.

One of the many people who were impressed and motivated by Phil Graham's energy and intelligence was Ben Bradlee, executive editor of the *Post* and *Newsweek*'s Washington bureau chief and later managing editor. In his 1995 autobiography, *A Good Life: Newspapering and Other Adventures,* Bradlee credited Phil Graham for leading *Newsweek* through a series of well-considered firings and hirings. But looking back, Bradlee also recalled:

> Phil dropped off our screen soon after the purchase of
> *Newsweek*, and we were so involved with ourselves . . .
> that we didn't worry about his absence. And we certainly
> didn't know the reason. We didn't know that Phil had
> suffered from severe depression since 1957, alternating
> between lows of withdrawal and dependency, and manic
> highs of erratic behavior and booze. It was his illness that
> had convinced many of his close friends that buying
> *Newsweek* would be ill-advised. Katharine herself had felt
> this way at first, then came to believe that the purchase
> would help assuage Phil's feeling that he was too much an
> overseer of her father Eugene Meyer's achievements, and
> not enough an architect of his own.

In the early 1960s Kay and Phil Graham both
became part of the circle of bright, privileged, and
powerful young Americans who socialized with and
near President Kennedy and his graceful wife, Jackie.
Years later, Katharine Graham still remembered "the
excitement and hope generated by a president who was
vibrant, young, eloquent, and committed to solving
old problems in new ways." But the high spirits of the
times weren't strong enough to completely counteract
the continuing troubles in the Graham household. Kay
came down with a case of tuberculosis, while Phil
continued to cycle in and out of depressions. When he
wasn't rushing around the office or jetting around the
country, he was back at home, talking to his wife for
hours about how miserable and hopeless he felt. His
tendency toward violent anger, once directed only at
Kay, started to reveal itself even at work, but his close
colleagues—honorable, loyal men like Russ Wiggins
and Al Friendly—covered for their friend. Most of the
people at the *Post* had no idea how often their boss
succumbed to terrible rages.

And then another factor entered into his already
complicated life: a young Australian journalist by the
name of Robin Webb. On Christmas Eve afternoon

in 1962, Katharine Graham picked up her home telephone, not realizing that Phil had already picked up the extension in another room. Kay overheard her husband speaking to Robin "in words that made the situation plain," according to her account of the experience in her memoir. She confronted her husband, and he admitted that he was having an affair. At first Phil said he wanted to preserve the marriage and the

Former president John F. Kennedy delivers a speech as Phil Graham looks on. Kennedy was one of many illustrious figures that the Grahams knew personally because of the couple's involvement with the Post.

family and promised that he would end the affair even though he admitted loving the young woman. A few weeks later, however, Phil abruptly changed his mind and moved out of the house to be with Robin.

Bradlee described his perspective on the situation in his biography:

> Phil had reemerged with a bang in 1962 when he showed up in New York, Paris, and Washington with Robin Webb, not Katharine Graham, on his arm. . . . She and Phil had stumbled from a fling to an affair when no one was noticing. But toward the end of 1962, Phil moved out of R Street [his family home] and set up shop with Robin, and everyone was noticing. All of Phil's old friends remained resolutely loyal to Katharine.

Katharine did not blame Robin for what was happening, believing the young woman was obviously charmed by Phil, and didn't understand the background. But Phil's friends and associates were beginning to see the bigger and darker picture. Phil was drunk nearly all the time these days. In Phoenix, Arizona, Phil got up to the podium to make a speech at an Associated Press meeting, but his remarks degenerated into nonsense and obscenities. "As with other outrageous behavior by noted or known persons in those days, the incident was hushed up and not reported," Katharine later wrote. Shortly after this incident, Phil committed another truly outrageous act by calling President Kennedy from his hotel room in Phoenix. Apparently, Phil and JFK were close enough acquaintances that the president actually took his call.

At this point, Phil's family and friends spun into action, hoping to intervene before Phil became more out of touch with his family and responsibilities. Two of Phil's children, Lally and Don, went out West to find their father, who had to be forcibly tranquilized by doctors before being put on a plane back to Washington. From there, he spent time at Georgetown

Washington University Hospital and was later transferred to Chestnut Lodge, a private mental hospital in
suburban Washington.

   After ten days at Chestnut Lodge and three days
with his ineffective private psychiatrist, Dr. Farber,
Phil took off again for New York. He hired a divorce
lawyer and started making plans to leave Katharine
and marry Robin. As if that was not egregious
enough, he was also angling to try to take total
control of the Washington Post Company. Katharine
was completely bewildered and offended. After all, it
was her father's financial backing that had enabled

*In 1963, Katharine and
friends began to worry about
Phil Graham's mental well-
being, and checked him into
Georgetown Washington
University Hospital (above).
Phil committed suicide a few
months later.*

the paper to survive all those years, and it was Kay's payment of all their marital living expenses that had allowed Phil to purchase his portion of the *Post* stock with his income. She described the trauma of the betrayal she felt: "In some ways, this was the bottom moment for me—very confusing, very difficult, and very painful. Not only had I lost my husband but I was about to lose the *Post*. I saw his plan as a logical aspect of his illness, and I knew he was really ill, but by now the effect was real and I was frightened." Despite her fears and growing despondency, Kay felt she had no choice but to fight for the paper, even though she doubted she had the ability to run it. When she expressed those doubts to a friend, her friend responded firmly. "Of course you can do it. . . . You've got all those genes. It's ridiculous to think you can't do it. You've just been pushed down so far you don't recognize what you can do."

The terrible double threat of losing both her husband and her family's legacy hung over Katharine Graham for months. Then, just as suddenly as he had left, Phil contacted his wife and announced that he wanted to come back. Relieved, Kay took him back and then set to work trying to get Phil the best medical attention available. She was still listening to the advice of Dr. Farber, whom she would later come to view as incompetent.

Katharine and everyone else in Phil's life wanted to believe he was better. Because of his mental illness, Phil's "true" self was a mystery to his own wife, as he was to everyone who loved and admired him. Ben Bradlee offered in his autobiography, "I never felt I knew Phil Graham, the way a man ought to know a friend. His mind was so fast; his wit so keen; his charm was subtle, yet tangible; he was the friend we all dreamed of having. And yet before the discovery of drugs that could have controlled his violent mood swings, he was doomed."

Tapping into his great gifts of charm and persuasion, Phil convinced the Chestnut Lodge doctors, who were once again in charge of his care, to let him come home for the weekend. Clearly, he was planning all along to get back to his country house, where his guns were kept. He managed to persuade everyone, including his doctors, children, wife of 23 years, that he was only looking for a short break from the rigors of the mental hospital. In truth, he had carefully planned and plotted his permanent break from the pain he was suffering. This eloquent and intelligent man left no suicide note.

According to Katharine's memoir, President Kennedy had once remarked about his good friend Phil Graham, "The line is too damn narrow between rationality and irrationality in Phil." Phil's final act exemplified the truth of that statement.

The early 1960s was a transition period for Katharine Graham, as she worked through the tragedy of her husband's suicide and adapted to the task of managing a major newspaper.

5

LEARNING TO LEAD

Katharine Graham was accustomed to thinking of herself as a caretaker of others, first and foremost. So in the weeks after Phil's death, when it came time for her to take the reins of the Washington Post Company as its new president, she was not really focused on her potential power in the role. Instead, she was thinking in terms of her duties to the next generation of Grahams. She revealed in her memoir that she saw herself "as a bridge to my children," who would eventually take over the enterprise.

In his autobiography, Ben Bradlee noted that most of Kay's friends and colleagues at the paper secretly wanted her to sell the *Post*. Once it was clear that she would never sell, she was expected to play a merely symbolic role at the head of the company. It took Graham months, Bradlee noted, before she became confident enough to assert to others that she planned to be more than a figurehead.

Because she had so much to learn about the business, Katharine Graham did not envision herself as the one who would be making major decisions about the *Post*, *Newsweek*, and the company's growing TV and radio broadcasting division. Instead, she planned to play a supporting role to the many adept men whom Phil had hired to run the various divisions of the company. Graham admitted:

> I naively thought the whole business would just go on as it had while I learned by listening. I didn't realize that nothing stands still—issues arise every day, big and small, and they start coming at you. I didn't understand the immensity of what lay before me, how frightened I would be by much of it, how tough it was going to be, and how many anxious hours and days I would spend for a long, long time. Nor did I realize how much I was eventually going to enjoy it all.

Graham did not come equipped with a lot of in-depth knowledge about the business, but at least she had some firsthand understanding of and appreciation for news reporting. From her years of marriage to the *Post*'s publisher, she knew the principal journalists fairly well and had often discussed the news and the company with them.

Katharine rapidly realized that her larger-than-life husband would be a tough act to follow. She saw that she had always had a tendency to mythologize Phil, but now she became aware that his colleagues and employees often idealized him as well. At the beginning of her tenure as head of the company, she still felt like she was living in his shadow. "I didn't have as much energy as Phil had had, nor were my interests as broad, my knowledge nearly as deep, or my training as adequate," she said. "What I essentially did was to put one foot in front of the other, shut my eyes, and step off the edge. The surprise was that I landed on my feet."

Eventually Kay did start to recognize that Phil, for all his brilliance and hard work, wasn't perfect—especially in those last few years of his illness. As Bradlee recalled, "No one can imagine how difficult it was for the *Post*'s managers—editors and business types—to cope with Phil Graham's illness in the last long months of his manic depression. Many of them were fired, then rehired. Many were confronted with decisions taken by Phil—a new bureau here, a new executive there— pursuant to priorities and judgments that were at least erratic." Still, many people genuinely loved Phil, and Katharine found herself comforting those who would stop by her office to express their grief over his loss.

She was fortunate to receive great support from people within the organization—particularly Fritz Beebe, a lawyer who was also relatively new at the media business but had served as Phil's right-hand man—and from her network of friends and family. Graham's daughter Lally, although back at college, offered an incredible amount of comfort and love in the first difficult weeks and months. In one remarkably clearheaded letter to her mother, Lally wrote,

> There is no use in my again reiterating my belief that you will do very well with the business—as we agreed not in a Daddy way for who else in the world could run things with his brilliance and imagination—yet in another way, your own, which in a different way will be just as good— your good judgment, great ability to get along with people, earn their respect and discern their strengths and weaknesses and desire to follow things up which Pa was quite unwilling to do.

Katharine was completely ignorant about some basic facts of the working world: the proper way to give praise and criticism and the way to manage time effectively, for example. She was not aware of such tools as "headhunter" companies, which are contracted to find and hire executive employees. She started to annoy the other executives and managers with her tendency to ask a lot of questions. In her enthusiasm to learn, she did not realize that her inquisitive, humble, deferential demeanor actually generated a lack of confidence in her abilities as a leader.

Post publisher John Sweeterman, who had worked side by side with Phil Graham in developing the business strategy of the company for more than 10 years, was particularly aggravated by Kay Graham's questions. In her memoir, she provided readers with an analysis of the cause of her tense relationship with Sweeterman: "From 1961, when he had been made publisher, but especially since the onset of Phil's more pronounced ups and downs, John had been the final decision-maker, consulting no one, conferring with few about his decisions. And here I came along, asking hundreds of questions." She was Sweeterman's boss, but her questions proved to him that she didn't know the business well, yet.

Despite problems like the one with Sweeterman, Graham was beginning to win supporters among her colleagues and managed to gain sound advice from several of them. Star reporter Walter Lippmann, for example, wrote her a letter explaining how to manage the deluge of reading material that the owner of a major newspaper was expected to digest on a daily basis. He proposed that Graham spend no more than an hour each morning reading articles and skimming headlines. For the important or interesting stories, Lippman suggested, she should then call a brief meeting with the reporters involved and have them explain the topic and give her an update. In this way she could most efficiently lead the paper. She would be informed of the news of the day while developing a relationship with the paper's reporters and editors.

For every bit of good advice and support she received, Graham was subjected to all sorts of subtle and not-so-subtle messages about her unsuitability for the job. She loathed attending board meetings or conferences where she would be the only woman in the room. The speaker would start the presentation by saying, with a smirk and a giggle, "Lady and gentlemen"

While getting settled as the new publisher of the Washington Post, *Graham found help and advice from staff members like renowned columnist Walter Lippmann.*

or "Gentlemen and Mrs. Graham." At one meeting, a male friend of Katharine was moderating a discussion about an issue that was, she admitted, totally new to her. He went around the room, gathering opinions on the topic from every man in the room, but passed over Kay completely. Katharine began to notice that often-times in a business setting, women seemed invisible to men, "who looked right through you as though you weren't there." She made the grave mistake of mentioning her observations and feelings of frustration to one of *Newsweek*'s executives, a man she thought she could trust, apparently. This man reacted to her observation with annoyance to her sensitivity, and he no longer invited her to important meetings.

Nevertheless, she was in a position of great power and influence, whether she fully realized it or not. After so many years in which her children's welfare and her husband's ill health had completely dominated her vision, Katharine Graham's view of the world began to expand rapidly. She started attending editorial meetings and lunches, which involved informal discussions between reporters and the important political or cultural figures they covered. In her autobiography, Graham described an episode that illustrated her early sense of insecurity at these meetings:

> I remember one very early editorial lunch—when I was still painfully unsure of myself—at which our guest was Madame Nhu, the sinister, powerful sister-in-law of South Vietnamese President Ngo Dinh Diem. She was . . . widely feared and disliked. This was the first lunch at which I asked a question, and I almost collapsed from worry as I summoned up my courage to ask it. I have no memory of what I actually asked, but I have a very vivid recollection of nearly dying afterwards from embarrassment and fear that I had looked stupid or ignorant.

She decided to throw her weight into the news business, which meant learning how to use her best judgment with confidence to navigate through various political and ethical muddles. After President Kennedy's assassination in November 1963, Graham became quite friendly with his successor, former vice president Lyndon B. Johnson, or LBJ—the aggressive, charismatic, and masterful politician from Texas, whom Phil had respected. Katharine also developed a warm rapport with LBJ's gracious wife, Claudia "Lady Bird" Johnson. When LBJ was up for reelection in 1964, he courted endorsements from the press, including the *Washington Post*.

Katharine Graham and Lyndon B. Johnson had been friends since 1961, when he was the vice-presidential running mate with the Democratic presidential candidate John F. Kennedy.

Although Kay Graham counted herself as a supporter on a personal level, she was determined to stick to the newspaper's policy of remaining independent, or nonpartisan, which means being not explicitly in favor of one political party or another. In the spirit of neutrality, Graham decided to write a long letter to LBJ's Republican opponent, Senator Barry Goldwater, inviting him to a "get acquainted" luncheon with the editorial staffs of the *Post* and *Newsweek*. Commenting years later, Graham recalled that she made the invitation because she believed that the *Post* had to remain fair, detached, and as objective as possible in its news reporting.

On a visit to LBJ's ranch in Austin, Texas, Katharine tried to explain her position without offending the president:

> I . . . said that I admired the legislation he himself had got passed and was for him and wanted to make sure he knew it. Although we had a policy at the *Post* against contributing to campaigns, it had been followed loosely. Phil hadn't actually contributed to campaigns, but I had. I guess I forgot I was now in the other seat, because I told the president that my mother and I both wanted to contribute to his campaign. Later, I came to believe that the paper had to be completely neutral, and I decided never to make another contribution to a presidential campaign.

LBJ, who was known for occasional outbursts of temper, actually accepted Graham's position graciously, indicating that he had appreciated her help in the past. But in her recollections from nearly a half-century later, Katharine admitted that the newspaper's policy of non-endorsement had actually hurt LBJ deeply. He couldn't understand why he had not received the liberal *Washington Post*'s endorsement when he had earned the support of Republican and even right-wing papers. Nevertheless, Graham had made up her mind to stick to her guns on this matter. It was one of the first of many decisive moments to come—but such strongly held, potentially divisive positions did not come easy to her. She wrote:

> Women traditionally . . . have suffered—and many still do—from an exaggerated desire to please, a syndrome so instilled in women of my generation that it inhibited my behavior for many years, and in ways still does. Although at the time I didn't realize what was happening, I was unable to make a decision that might displease those around me. For years, whatever directive I may have issued ended with the phrase "if it's all right with you."

This was her considered opinion on her own past, observed from the distance of decades. At the time,

Graham did not view circumstances in these general terms. She was so focused on her own feelings of inadequacy and incompetence that she did not recognize these perceptions as a problem faced by many women in many walks of life.

As a result of being the only woman in charge of a major U.S. newspaper, Katharine herself became newsworthy. Calling the experience a "strange and difficult" one, she first found herself a topic of media interest in 1963, as several magazines and newspapers asked to interview her. Over the next few years, she

During her career, Katharine was associated with many famous writers such as novelist Truman Capote. This picture was taken from a party thrown by Capote in 1966.

became proficient in being interviewed. Her old acquaintance Arthur Schlesinger Jr. profiled Graham in a piece for *Vogue*; soon afterward, she appeared on the covers of the magazines *Business Week* and *Washingtonian*. The profiles were generally very positive and often quite flattering. In retrospect, however, Graham realized that these interviews revealed a large and persistent blind spot in her thinking, as she commented in her autobiography:

> In one published interview, I said I did not find it difficult to be a woman executive in a field dominated by men, and "after a while, people forget you're a woman." That last was bravura, brought on by my newness and inexperience. Women's issues hadn't yet surfaced, and I simply wasn't sensitive to how people viewed me. Since I was so painfully new and had so much to learn, the unpleasantness of being condescended to and the strangeness of being the only woman in so many rooms got mixed up in my mind.

In another interview as late as 1969, Katharine even expressed that she could not imagine a woman acting as managing editor of a newspaper. As for her own position as both the Washington Post Company president and the *Washington Post* publisher (the latter title was given to her that year, after John Sweeterman quit the paper), Graham reflected, "I think a man would be better at this job I'm in than a woman." After that interview appeared in the fashion industry newspaper *Women's Wear Daily*, Graham's friend, Elsie Carpenter, a longtime reporter and editor at the *Post*, marched into her boss's office and said, "Do you really believe that? Because, if you do, I quit."

Startling moments like these were beginning to shake Katharine out of her unquestioned assumptions about male and female roles. By the early 1970s, with the encouragement of the women's movement and

the goading of her friend and prominent feminist leader Gloria Steinem, Graham began to develop a heightened sensitivity to women's issues. She argued when the *Newsweek* editors refused to consider an experienced art critic named Aline Saarinen for an editorial position simply because she was female— although Graham ultimately backed down.

Katharine eventually began to understand and acknowledge that the battle for workplace equality was personal as well as professional, and that all the slights, insults, and unfairness she experienced in her "top dog" position were a reflection of the troubles women were facing at all ranks in the company. In 1970, 46 women at *Newsweek* filed a complaint with a federal agency, the Equal Employment Opportunity Commission (EEOC), claiming discrimination. Later

Katharine Graham presents the first Paris edition of the New York Herald Tribune-The Washington Post *in 1966. As president of the* Post, *Graham was always interested in expanding the Washington Post Company through international business ventures.*

on, the *Post* was also sued. Complaints from women regarding sex discrimination were eventually followed by complaints from blacks and other minorities charging racial bias in hiring and promotions. These developments served as another jolt to Graham's thinking, as well as to the thinking of a few other fair-minded people in the company.

In his autobiography, Bradlee admitted that during his first few years as managing editor of the *Post*, almost all the newly hired reporters were white men, rising stars such as Ward Just, who covered Vietnam memorably, and David Broder, whom Bradlee called "the greatest pure political reporter of his generation." There were very few women on the editorial staff and only one or two black men at any one time, which many would perceive as a truly scandalous situation in a city with a majority black population.

Bradlee explained that during the Second World War many women reporters took the places of male reporters who went off to fight in or cover the war. Although many of them had excelled as skilled journalists, most were forced to resign from their posts after the war as a law went into effect that guaranteed returning veterans the same jobs they held when they went to war. "News magazines were siphoning off good young talent, males and females, much as television had done in the decade from 1955 to 1965. This is an explanation, not an excuse. I was not sensitive to racism or sexism, to understate the matter."

Despite the increased attention to such issues, it took people like Graham and Bradlee a long time to put into effect their strengthening ideals about equality and fairness in the workplace. In the beginning, their efforts, as Katharine depicted in her autobiography, to hire 'qualified' women and minorities were carried out inadequately. "When saddled with inadequate talent or failures whether women or blacks, we didn't know either how to work with them to bring them along or how to let them go. Eventually things improved dramatically at both places, but without the suits and without the [equal opportunity] laws adopted by the country, this would have happened even more slowly."

Katharine Graham and Ben Bradlee, executive editor of the Post, *leave the U.S. District Court in Washington, D.C., on June 21, 1971, rejoicing over the court's decision to permit the newspaper to publish the controversial Pentagon Papers.*

6

BREAKING THROUGH TO THE NEXT LEVEL

Throughout Graham's early years as president of the Washington Post Company, the United States was becoming increasingly involved in a terrible conflict taking place on the other side of the globe in a small nation known as Vietnam. Formerly a French colony known as Indochina, the country of Vietnam had fought bitterly for its independence throughout the 1940s and 1950s. At the end of this war, the country was divided into North Vietnam—under the control of Vietnamese Communists who had opposed French rule and who sought a unified communist government over the whole country—and South Vietnam—under the control of those who had sympathized with French rule and had collaborated with France. This all took place during the height of the cold war era between the United States and the Soviet Union—the same period that gave rise to a Western concern over the threat of the continued spread of communism, which spawned with it the paranoia of McCarthyism. Under a belief known as "the domino theory," many U.S. diplomats and politicians feared that if Vietnam fell entirely under the rule of the North Vietnamese rulers, then communism would spread throughout Southeast Asia and beyond.

In 1946, the United States and France began involving themselves in the civil war between North and South Vietnam. The United States eventually wielded a great deal of behind-the-scenes power there and in 1955 played a decisive role (and arguably an illegal one by the conventions of international law) by installing a new leader, Ngo Dinh Diem, at the head of the anticommunist regime in South Vietnam. It is widely believed that the election that put Diem into office—with 98.2 percent of the vote—was rigged.

Diem turned out to be a violently repressive leader, whose supporters were mostly wealthy and powerful people and allies of the old French colonial government. A growing opposition to Diem's regime within South Vietnam convinced President Lyndon B. Johnson that the United States needed to send military advisors and financial assistance to hold the Diem government in power, the bastion against a communist-ruled Vietnam. By mid-1964, LBJ had sent 27,000 "advisors"—actually soldiers—to Vietnam. Over the next few years, U.S. involvement would escalate into a full-scale, deadly war with the North Vietnam armies. Ultimately, by the war's end in 1975, more than half a million American men would serve, over 58,000 Americans would eventually lose their lives, and more than 300,000 would come home wounded. Coupled with this growing involvement was an increasingly bitter antiwar movement back in the United States—demonstrations, teach-ins, sit-ins, and a few violent rallies in which students and other activists were hurt or killed.

During his campaign to succeed LBJ as president of the United States, Richard M. Nixon announced that he had a secret plan to end the war. In 1969, President Nixon issued what came to be called the Nixon Doctrine, announcing that U.S. troops would no longer directly involve themselves in Asian wars. However, forced to renege, he authorized secret bombings in Vietnam and sent more troops back in to fight an increasingly unpopular war.

Against this volatile backdrop, Katharine Graham,

U.S. soldiers stand ready in a field in South Vietnam. As the Vietnam War dragged on into the 1970s, the Post *and other newspapers reported on the decline of public support for U. S. involvement in the conflict.*

still unsure of herself as a leader, made a decision that would help push the *Washington Post* into the upper echelons of world-class journalism. Although the newspaper had grown and matured enormously under Phil's watch, it was still struggling to secure admiration and respect in the field. Concerning the *Post*'s reputation before the late 1960s, Ben Bradlee remarked, "There was not yet a steady diet of good stories. The paper still was hard to read. Production quality was a disgrace, with typos galore, with color so bad that the people in pictures regularly had four eyes and two sets of teeth. The design was just plain ugly." For decades, *The New York Times* had been considered the "paper of record," the final news authority not just for metropolitan New York City but also for the United States and, increasingly, the whole planet. But after Graham's momentous and risky decision in 1971, and the positive developments that directly resulted from it, people would start referring to the *Times* and the *Post* in the same respectful breath. Paradoxically, the watershed moment for the *Post* came directly out of having been "scooped"—i.e., beaten to a breaking story— by the *Times*.

The publication of this exclusive story turned out to be a key event in turning public opinion finally and definitively against the war in Vietnam. Daniel Ellsberg, a senior analyst at the U.S. Department of Defense, had secretly compiled and brought to the *Times* photocopies of classified official government documents that showed a clear pattern of deception toward the public. On a Sunday in June, the New York newspaper published six full pages of news stories and top-secret documents showing, in effect, how President Johnson and his military advisors had secretly escalated the war effort without congressional or legal backing. A few days later, the U.S. Justice Department went to court and got

an injunction against the *Times*—a court order restraining the newspaper from publishing any further information based on Ellsberg's leaked documents, now known as the Pentagon Papers. As Graham explained in her memoir, "This was America's first-ever order for prior restraint of the press."

While the lawyers for the *New York Times* went to work to try to reverse the gag order, Ben Bradlee and the *Post*'s national editor, Ben Bagdikian, con-trived to get their own copy of the Pentagon Papers

Dr. Daniel Ellsberg (left), who provided the press with the Pentagon Papers, was charged in 1971 with illegal possession of secret government papers. Ellsberg defended his actions by stating that the country had a right to know exactly how U.S. leaders were handling national affairs during the Vietnam War.

from Daniel Ellsberg. Bradlee detailed the procedure in his autobiography: "Late Wednesday, the 16th, Bagdikian flew to Boston, and first thing Thursday morning, he flew back with two first-class seats, one for himself and one for a large cardboard carton full of Pentagon Papers"—about 4,000 pages out of the total 7,000 that the *Times* had received.

Katharine was immensely pleased that the *Post* had these groundbreaking documents in hand. But the *Post*'s lawyers were not so elated. Fritz Beebe, a lawyer and longtime friend and ally of the Graham family, worried that publishing such damaging reports was somehow contrary to the good of the country as well as the company. The Washington Post Company was in a particularly sensitive spot, since it was about to "go public," i.e., become a publicly owned entity with its stock owned by outside investors and traded on Wall Street. "Fritz had an extraordinary sensitivity to editorial issues and to the editors themselves . . . but in this case, as a lawyer, he had to worry about the future of the company," Graham explained. Fritz Beebe was particularly frightened that the government would prosecute the newspaper under the Espionage Act, reducing the company to the status of a felon, which would mean its licenses to own and operate its television stations would be stripped.

Kay found herself squeezed between the editors and reporters who solidly supported publication on the grounds of "freedom of the press" and the lawyers who cautioned against the legal ramifications of publication. The deadline for the next morning's first edition of the paper had passed, and the deadline for the second edition was quickly approaching. Everyone was looking to her to make the final call, and she was not at all sure what to do. Graham was especially troubled by the fact that

Fritz was advising against publishing the Pentagon Papers:

> I knew him so well, and we had never differed on any important issue; and, after all, he was the lawyer, not I. But I also heard *how* he said it; he didn't hammer at me, he didn't stress the issues related to going public, and he didn't say the obvious thing—that I would be risking the whole company on this decision. He simply said he guessed he wouldn't. I felt that, despite his stated opinion, he had somehow left the door open for me to decide on a different course. Frightened and tense, I took a big gulp and said, "Go ahead, go ahead, go ahead. Let's go. Let's publish."

The *Post* ran its own Pentagon Paper coverage the next day, filling the gaps in the story that the *Times* was barred against publishing. Katharine's decision did indeed result in an action by the Justice Department against the Washington Post Company. The next few days were a whirlwind of anxiety for Graham and all her colleagues. During the rest of June 1971, the cases against the *New York Times* and the *Washington Post* proceeded all the way up the chain of our court system, until at last, the U.S. Supreme Court ruled in favor of the newspapers, 6–3. The court ruled that no compelling national interest would be threatened by the publication of the truth.

In retrospect, Ben Bradlee wondered, "What the hell was going on in this country that this could happen?" Eighteen years afterward, Bradlee noted, one of the judges involved in the cases confessed, "I have never seen any trace of a threat to the national security from the Pentagon Papers' publication." Yet the publication was a powerful moment: soon after the Johnson administration's deceptions had been revealed, support for Nixon's war policies

A pressman proudly holds up the Post *edition covering a U.S. Supreme Court ruling on June 30, 1971, that acknowledged the newspaper's right to publish the Pentagon Papers.*

plummeted, with polls showing that 60 percent of the public now considered the war "immoral" and 70 percent demanded an immediate withdrawal from Vietnam. The majority of Americans finally got what they wanted in 1975.

Back at the *Post*, the experience of publishing the Pentagon Papers forged a new bond between

Katharine Graham, the executives, and the editorial staff. As Bradlee described the climate, there was now "a sense of mission and agreement of new goals, and how to attain them. . . . After the Pentagon Papers, there would be no decision too difficult for us to overcome together." For Graham as an individual and leader, the experience was a galvanizing one. She and her newspaper had burst onto the national scene in such a way that she herself came to believe in her decision-making ability. This boost in confidence would come in handy for Graham during the next major U.S. political upheaval: the complex, multilayered scandal known as Watergate.

*Graham's newspaper made history with its coverage of the 1972 Watergate scandal,
which eventually led to the resignation of President Richard Nixon. Sitting on her
desk is an issue of* Newsweek *that covered the scandal.*

7

RIGHT PLACE, RIGHT TIME

Even more so than most other U.S. presidents in the 20th century, Richard Milhaus Nixon hated the press. He would eventually grow to loathe the *Washington Post* in particular.

On June 17, 1972, five men wearing surgical gloves were caught breaking into the headquarters of the Democratic National Committee at the Watergate apartment and office complex in downtown Washington, D.C. The next day, the *Post* reported that the presumed burglars were trying to plant "bugs" (special wiring used to listen in secretly to telephone conversations). President Nixon's press secretary dismissed the incident, warning that "certain elements" might try to stretch the story beyond the truth. In the end, however, the arrest of the burglars uncovered a White House-sponsored plan of spying against political opponents and a trail of guilt that led to many top-ranking political officials and to Nixon himself.

The president's associates had been pursuing a massive, nationwide campaign of spying and sabotage on behalf of Nixon for his upcoming reelection efforts. When all was said and done, several key figures would be sentenced to prison and several witnesses would make scandalous revelations about the Nixon White House. Under oath during a Senate hearing a year after the burglary, White House counsel John Dean testified that Attorney General John Mitchell had ordered the break-in and a subsequent cover-up of any White House involvement. It was also later revealed that since 1971 a White House group called the "plumbers" had been doing whatever was necessary to stop leaks to the press—including a break-in at the office of Daniel Ellsberg's psychiatrist, in an attempt to find personal information that would impugn Ellsberg and discredit his decision to leak the Pentagon Papers.

Soon thereafter, White House aide Alexander Butterfield unlocked the entire investigation with his testimony. He told the Senate, on national television, that Nixon had ordered a taping system installed in the White House to record all conversations automatically. Nixon was then ordered to release the tapes, but he refused. After much political and legal wrangling, Nixon was forced to turn over the tapes. Although there were several key conversations missing and a mysterious 18-1/2-minute gap on one tape, it became clear that Nixon had been involved in punishing and sabotaging political opponents and in trying to thwart the Watergate investigations. Further investigations also revealed that the Nixon administration had solicited large amounts of illegal campaign contributions, $500,000 of which was used to pay the Watergate burglars. In the ensuing political turmoil, Nixon chose to resign from the presidency rather than face an impeachment hearing.

As Katharine Graham offered 20 years later, "None of us, of course, had any idea how far the story would stretch; the beginning—once the laughter died down—all seemed so farcical." The burglary at the DNC was just the tip of the iceberg.

Richard Nixon's presidency during the Vietnam era suffered much criticism; public opinion further plummeted with the breaking of the Post's *Watergate story.*

As she explained in her autobiography,

> we might never have known the size of the iceberg had it not been for the extraordinary investigative and reporting efforts of [Bob] Woodward and [Carl] Bernstein, famous names now but then two young men who had never worked together, one whom (Woodward) had not even been long at the paper. In some ways it was a natural pairing, since their qualities and skills complemented each other. Both are bright, but Woodward was conscientious, hardworking, and driven, and Bernstein messy and undisciplined. He was, however, the better writer, more imaginative and creative. In other ways the relationship was oil and water, but the end product came out right, despite—or perhaps because of—the strange mix.

Although the entire city staff of the paper contributed to the emerging story, Woodward and

Reporters Carl Bernstein (left) and Bob Woodward sit in the Post *newsroom. The two reporters broke the historic Watergate scandal story in 1972. They later won a Pulitzer Prize for their articles for the* Post.

Bernstein were the lead reporters who ferreted out all kinds of arcane pieces of information from hundreds of sources, including an anonymous tipster who came to be known as "Deep Throat." (These two would eventually write a best-selling book about Watergate, *All the President's Men,* which would be scripted for a movie starring Robert Redford as Woodward and Dustin Hoffman as Bernstein.) On the editorial page, writers Phil Geyelin and Meg Greenfield argued consistently about the utter seriousness of the unfolding story despite the fact that the White House had discounted the event. Herblock also kept up a relentless assault on the matter through his trenchant, critical cartoons.

Although many people criticized the paper for pursuing "a minor peccadillo, the sort of thing engaged in by lots of politicians," Graham and her staff stuck to the belief that there was a story behind Watergate, that the event was an attempt to subvert the political process. She later described the incident as an example of the "pervasive, indiscriminate use of power and authority from an administration with a passion for secrecy and deception and an astounding lack of regard for the normal constraints of democratic politics."

It was an exciting time for the paper, but also an anxious one. Nixon and other Republicans accused the *Post* of being "out to get" the president, in order to help support his Democratic opponent, George McGovern, in the upcoming election. Republican senator Bob Dole went around the country making speeches accusing the newspaper of relinquishing its objectivity and "set[ting] up housekeeping with the McGovern campaign," as Graham recalled. Political pressure was put on the Federal Communications Commission (FCC) to deny the Washington Post Company a renewal of its radio station operating licenses—a challenge that the company's lawyers had to spend several million dollars trying to beat. During this period, the stock price of the company went down from about $38 to about $17, effectively decreasing the value of the company by more than half. At one point, one of Graham's friends even warned her "not to be alone," as if the Nixon people might actually do her physical harm. She thought this was ridiculously overdramatic, but he insisted

Graham speaks at a meeting in January 1973 shortly after exposure of the Water-gate scandal won the Post *worldwide fame.*

that she take special precautions for her personal safety. Graham recounted that her friend "never explained what his fears were based on, and I still have no idea what he had heard or even meant, but I certainly got the point about how serious he was." Remembering these heady times, Graham emphasized how careful and responsible the newspaper tried to be in its reporting of the story:

> From the outset, the editors had resolved to handle the story with more than the usual scrupulous attention to fairness and detail. They laid down certain rules, which were followed by everyone. First, every bit of information attributed to an unnamed source had to be supported by at least one other, independent source. Particularly at the start of Watergate, we had to rely heavily on confidential sources, but at every step we double-checked every bit of material before printing it; where possible, we had three or even more sources for each story. Second, we ran nothing that was reported by any other newspaper, television, radio station, or other media outlet unless it was independently verified and confirmed by our own reporters. Third, every word of every story was read by at least one of the senior editors before it went into print.

In other words, Graham, Bradlee, and the *Post* staff were unflinchingly committed to getting to the truth of this major political scandal. The process of fighting off the newspaper's enemies and detractors pushed Katharine to a new level of maturity as a leader. She had come a long way from the apologetic, insecure, deferential creature she had been just a few years earlier.

Graham sits in the Post's *pressroom while reading a new edition of the paper. Many disputes would take place in this room during the 1980s, as relations between* Post *workers and management became strained.*

8

LABOR PAINS

Kay Graham always had great sympathy for labor unions. Her pro-labor views were in part inherited from her father, Eugene, who believed in the necessity of strong, healthy trade unionism and was the only publisher made an honorary member of the local union of pressmen (the workers who operated the printing presses). Graham had grown up during a strong period for the labor movement and had early on aspired to be a labor reporter. Therefore, it was particularly frustrating and painful for her to find herself in the early 1970s portrayed as the number one enemy of unions, particularly of Local 6—the very organization that had honored her father.

Trade unions, or guilds, are organizations that serve to represent and protect the rights of workers in skilled trades or occupations. Throughout the several centuries of their existence in Europe and the Americas, unions have brought about many honorable and necessary changes to the conditions in which their members work—decent wages, reasonable working hours and meaningful time off, protection from being fired without justification, and so on. Arguably, unions helped create a burgeoning middle class. In past eras, the owners of business enterprises, in conjunction with national or local governments, generally tried to suppress unionism through antiunion laws or through violence and espionage. In the United States, beginning in the early part of the 20th century, unions grew in power and eventually were recognized as a legal means for workers to band together and protect their rights for safe working conditions and job security. Unions use strikes (deliberate work stoppages) and collective bargaining (negotiations) as tools to gain increased wages or improved working conditions for their members.

In theory, the power of unions to interfere with a company's profit-making operations serves a natural counterbalance to the power of a company to exploit its workers in the name of profit. Ideally, the natural tension between labor unions and company owners/managers leads to healthy, fair compromises on both ends. But in practice, unions have sometimes become corrupt entities in their own right and have abused their power to achieve goals that a reasonable person might consider unfair, unjust— even exploitative.

Over many decades at the *Post*, a volatile combination of honorable intentions, honest mistakes, and naked greed and power-mongering resulted in a thorny internal war between management and labor. Like most big-city papers, the *Post* had become heavily unionized. A large percentage of employees, particularly in the production side, belonged to one of 13 unions representing craftsmen such as printers, machinists, paper-handlers, and so on. There was also a professional guild to which all newspaper reporters belonged. To get the paper written, laid out, printed, and distributed every day of the year without fail required the vigilant cooperation of all these various skilled workers. Beginning in the late 1960s and early

1970s, several unions encouraged their members to stage slowdowns or strikes in an effort to get better wages or other advantages. Some demands were fair, but others, perhaps, were unreasonable. For example, an old contract between management and the printers included a strange category of work known as "reproduce" or "bogus." These were typeset ads that had been received from large national advertisers. A decades-old clause in the union contract required that, although these ads were already in final form, they had to be re-typeset by the printers and then proofed, corrected, and reprinted. Then this duplicated work would be thrown away.

By the late 1960s, there were literally thousands of pages that had not yet gone through the "reproduce" process and were accumulating. The union refused any attempts to rewrite the contract to eliminate this completely useless work, because it meant that the *Post* would have to hire any printer who showed up and wanted a job since there would always be this theoretical backlog of work to do. "This was their gravy train," Graham recalled. "As long as we had reproduce . . . waiting to be set, any printer could arrive . . . and declare he was going to work for us. We could do nothing to stop the influx of unneeded typesetters and had scores of these printers who just stood around and drank or played the numbers. One man went around all day sucking an orange—full of vodka."

Alongside the problem of the printers and their "bogus" work, there were the pressmen, a tough, blue-collar, all-white, all-male union whose members, according to Graham, were in the habit of purposely slowing down their work and sabotaging the pressroom in one way or another in order to have to stay late and make large overtime wages. Up in the newsroom, the Newspaper Guild's members presented a similar set of problems. Graham was frustrated because the *Post*'s unit of the guild had one of the highest pay scales in the country. Because of the guild's many restrictive rules, it was almost impossible for management to fire someone unless proven guilty of lying, cheating, or stealing. Members of the union who were incompetent or lazy were immune from being fired.

In her early years at the paper, Graham had tried to develop a civil, even friendly rapport with union leaders, such as Jim Dugan, who headed up the pressmen, and Charlie Davis, who led the stereotypers. But as the years wore on, the demands voiced by these men, she believed, grew increasingly hostile and unfair. Although she theoretically respected the right for workers to strike, Katharine was now seeing the dark side of the labor movement.

In the early 1970s, she did her best to lead her executives and employees through several contract negotiations and strikes. Emergency procedures were put into place: salespeople and other white-collar employees who normally had nothing to do with the production process were trained to run the printing presses in case of a work stoppage by the craftsmen. Ben Bradlee, Meg Greenfield (deputy editor of the editorial page), and other relatively high-up editorial personnel would pitch in at all levels of the process. At one point, during a strike of the newspaper guild, Graham found herself working in the classified department, taking incoming ads from car dealers over the phone.

Eventually several of the conflicts between labor and management reached settlement. A new printers' contract in the fall of 1974 even ended the ridiculous practice of "reproduce" once and for all. However, there were more troubles. On October 1, 1975, at about 4:45 in the morning, Graham was awakened by a phone call from one of the younger *Post* executives, Mark Meagher, who had bad news: at the expiration of their current contract, the pressmen first indicated that they would not be going on strike, but then did so anyway at four in the morning, in the middle of a production run to get the next day's paper printed. Their exit was a violent one, during which they set fire to one of the presses and beat up the pressroom foreman. They then formed a loud and angry picket line outside the building.

When Graham arrived at about five in the morning and carefully made her way through the picketers and into the building, she was shocked and upset by the sight of the pressroom. She described the scene in her memoir: "Clearly there had been a riot of sorts. A foot of water covered the floor. The smell of smoke was everywhere. Ben later described the place as looking like 'the engineer room in a burned-out ship's hulk.'"

This was the first day of a strike that would last for a full five months and would threaten to kill off the *Washington Post* for good. In the first few days, with the equipment in disrepair, the emergency procedures to have nonunion personnel work the presses were irrelevant. The newspaper actually missed an entire day on October 2, but Mark, Katharine, her son Don—now a rising-star executive at the paper—and other executives scrambled for alternative solutions. Ultimately they hired a helicopter to land on the roof of the building (thereby avoiding the picket line) to pick up the typeset pages and transport them to outside printing shops. The people brave enough to cross the picket line—including members of the Newspaper Guild, who were torn between their sympathies for the pressmen's union and their loyalty to Graham and, most of all, to Bradlee—spent months on end doing a full two jobs: their own customary work during the day (as reporters, editors, salespeople, etc.), and then pitching in on some part of the printing/production process all night. Meanwhile, Katharine's legal and operations executives worked hard to reach an agreement with the vituperative and confrontational union. Many employees left their homes and literally set up camp within the offices. Graham arranged for three meals a day to be served in

Pressmen of the Local 6, a union representing many employees of the Post, *line up during a strike in December 1962. Relations with the pressmen would gradually worsen until Local 6 helped initiate the strike of 1975, which lasted a full five months and threatened to close down the newspaper.*

the company cafeteria. Somehow or another, with the help of loyal staffers, Kay and her colleagues managed never to miss another daily edition. Nevertheless, the paper was substantially thinner than normal and in great danger of folding altogether. Alerted to the strike, many advertisers had fled the *Post* and flocked to its main competitor, the *Washington Star*. This meant a loss of millions in revenue for the company.

The strike was an exceptionally bitter and violent one. Men and women who crossed the picket line to come into the building were in danger of being verbally assaulted or beaten up by the striking press-men and their supporters, including sympathetic members of other unions. Spouses of some of the nonstriking employees received threatening letters or phone calls from members of the union. Men like Jim Dugan and Charlie Davis, whom Graham had once considered friends, of a sort, went out in public and made personal, vicious attacks against Katharine and the organization. Rival newspaper the *Star* printed highly negative stories about Graham, portraying her (in a rather sexist manner) as a tempestuous, impossible-to-please tyrant and bully.

In the midst of all this, Katharine felt squeezed between competing interests: she was willing to negotiate a settlement with the union, but under no circumstances was she willing to hire back the men who had sabotaged and destroyed the press room. In December, the paper's executives delivered a pro-posed contract to the union, one that the company viewed as very generous to the pressmen. It included an increase in base pay—enough to make these workers the highest paid pressmen in the country—and other boons, but also ended certain practices that the company considered unfair. The union refused these terms.

Meanwhile, the publishers of other newspapers were eager to see the *Post* "bust" the union, which means to refuse to cooperate with the union altogether and replace striking union workers with new nonunion permanent workers. Because Graham still considered herself pro-labor and believed strongly in the right of certain trades to organize in this manner, this was not a solution she was eager to embrace. The *Post* ran a

Graham speaks to newsroom employees at a special Post *meeting during the 1975 pressmen's strike. Many reporters had to stand in for the pressmen while management tried to settle the labor dispute.*

full-page letter from Mark Meagher explaining its actions and also ran a classified ad for "immediate openings" in the pressroom. Both experienced and inexperienced applicants were welcomed. Katharine was astonished at the speed and number of responses from readers, as she related in her autobiography. "To our amazement, early the next morning there were about seven hundred people lined up in front of the building to be interviewed." Significantly, many of these people were African-Americans and other minorities, and several were women—so their arrival at the *Post* instantly reversed many decades of race and sex discrimination perpetuated by the all-white, all-male trade union.

Eventually, the strike came to an end as contract terms were agreed to. All the unions, with the exception of the pressmen, came back to work, and 22 of the pressmen quit the union to return to the *Post*. Many of them did so despite fear that the union would retaliate, according to Graham's revealing autobiography:

> I know that one of the supervisors who did come back, Hoot Gibson, was frightened at first. When I asked him what he thought might happen, or what the union could do to him, he responded, in his slow, West Virginia drawl, "Anything, anything at all. Why, they could kill your dog or your horse." Hoot and I had a long talk the morning he returned . . . about what had brought us to this dreadful mess. Hoot recalled the early days of the *Post*. . . . "We all enjoyed our work and each other." And he emphasized how much easier it was to relate to each other when the paper was smaller.

Although she had been appalled by the behavior of the pressmen and felt vindicated when seven of those directly responsible for the riots and sabotage were indicted on criminal charges by a federal grant jury, Graham knew that the company needed to change its policy in order to improve relations between management and labor. She recalled, "I take responsibility for some of the management problems that led to the eroding of our rights to run the pressroom; others I inherited. But wherever the source of the problems lay, I knew they had to be corrected. I was also convinced that we set about doing this in an enlightened and decent way."

The strike was a terrible tragedy in many ways: nearly 200 people lost their jobs, and one pressman committed suicide because he was too afraid to cross the picket line to go back to work. In the aftermath, Graham realized that the company now had a rare opportunity to start over with a clean slate. She and her executives could address various problems and inefficiencies in the production process, and they had gained the opportunity to deal more professionally with the unions. Katharine later admitted that the *Post* was fortunate to have survived the strike, but managed to do so with the help of leaders like Mark Meagher and Don Graham, and the nonunion members who helped get the paper out and delivered. The paper also benefited in some ways. The pressmen's choice to destroy the presses and behave violently, for example, actually ended up working in the company's favor, by shifting public opinion in favor of Katharine and her management team.

Kay Graham had been proud of the paper's previous big successes, most notably the publishing of the Pentagon Papers and Watergate coverage, but she understood that she had only an indirect impact in those events— the hardworking reporters and editors had been responsible for those achievements. However, weathering the dangerous strike was something she was willing to take at least some direct credit for. Drawing conclusions about the event and what was proved about her ability to lead, Graham remarked:

> It is ironic that I, who have never liked confrontations, should have been faced with this major one. My mother rarely did things tactfully or in a low-key way; she loved and thrived on strident confrontations. Perhaps for that reason, I always ran the other way when it came to a showdown. I hated fights, which I always found unpleasant and invariably feared losing. On the other hand, in this big one, when I was cornered, I had no choice to become embattled.

Graham was proud of her own decisions and actions during this period, but she remained grateful to many people. In particular, "those 125 *Post* people who worked so hard at their own jobs by day and other jobs by night, doing work normally done by nearly fifteen hundred full and part-time production people, earned my undying respect and affection. I have always considered the daily paper a miracle of sorts, but never more so than during a strike."

After Graham passed her duties as Post *publisher on to her son, Don, in 1979, she had more time to travel and meet with prominent figures. Here she attends a conference in 1982 with Indira Gandhi, at that time prime minister of India.*

9

HISTORY CONSIDERED, AND A LEGACY RENEWED

With the strike crisis behind her, Kay Graham felt vindicated in her role as leader of the Washington Post Company. Her confidence had grown over the years, and the corporation's various business operations—the *Post*, *Newsweek*, and several radio and TV stations, primarily—were generally experiencing growth and progress.

During the late 1970s and through the 1980s, there were several mini-crises, often having to do with the hiring or firing of top executives or with the constant pressure on a public organization like the Washington Post Company to demonstrate its value to Wall Street. There were also difficult moments for Graham personally. As her public profile rose considerably during the strike, she became the subject of news articles, not all of them flattering. One article printed in *Time* magazine—*Newsweek*'s chief competitor—described Katharine, as she remembered it, as "'difficult to get along with, mercurial, [and] impulsive.'" In response to the criticism, she said, "I particularly detested the sexist implications of stories like these—always

being depicted as the difficult woman, while who-
ever left the company was the victim of my female
whims. I was still a curiosity, a woman in a man's
world. Men [at the head of media companies] fired
executive after executive, but no one attributed their
actions to their gender."

Near the end of 1978, after 15 years of running the
Post, Katharine decided it was time to slow down.
Since 1971, her son Don had moved up the ranks
from metro reporter, to sports editor, to assistant
general manager. A Harvard graduate, Vietnam vet,
and former policeman for the District of Columbia,
Don had showed great promise as a newspaperman
from the very start of his career. The business was
clearly in his blood. Kay knew that Don was ready,
noting "he had always been more mature than his
years—always hardworking, conscientious, decent,
bright, and able." In January 1979, Donald Graham
was named publisher of the *Post*, while his mother
retained the titles of chairman and chief executive
officer of the Washington Post Company. She
explained, "I had withdrawal pangs, but I left with
a more-than-full-time and challenging job as head
of the company . . . responsible for the growth,
soundness, and economic health of a half-billion-
dollar company with five thousand employees and
about two thousand shareholders." She was also
eventually named president of the otherwise all-male
American Newspaper Publishers Association, which
brought with it a whole other set of responsibilities
and duties.

The 1980s were filled with various challenges in
both the business and editorial sides of the company.
Perhaps the most dramatic episode was the contro-
versy resulting from the Janet Cooke article of 1981.
A 26-year-old rising-star reporter named Janet Cooke
published an article on the front page of the *Post*
entitled "Jimmy's World," about an eight-year-old

heroin addict. The story was widely read and admired, as Graham depicted in her memoir:

> We felt the story was so good and so well written that we submitted it for a Pulitzer Prize, which it won. The day after the prize was announced, though, the whole story began to unravel, as it was revealed that there were inconsistencies and exaggerations—if not untruths—in the way Cooke had portrayed her own life. . . . [Eventually] Janet Cooke finally confessed to *Post* editors that she had fabricated the story. "Jimmy" turned out to be a composite, and the quotes attributed to the child were, in fact, invented.

In the aftermath, Cooke returned the Pulitzer Prize and handed in her resignation. Unfortunately, however, she refused to take full responsibility for her actions; according to Graham, she instead accused the paper of creating unhealthy competition among reporters to create sensational articles intended for the front page. In part, the accusation was fair: Watergate had indeed spawned a great desire among young, ambitious reporters to become the next Bob Woodward or Carl Bernstein.

The *Post* accepted some measure of responsibility. Graham admitted that the editorial staff had not followed through in checking the facts of the story: "Many things had indeed gone wrong. At almost no point was Cooke asked hard questions about what she was reporting. She was trusted, and she wrote so well that no one thought to check the facts of the story." But Graham was still annoyed by "the self-righteousness on the part of many in the [newspaper] industry, assuming it couldn't have happened in other places." And indeed, since that time, several noteworthy cases of plagiarism or false reporting at newspapers and magazines have made national headlines, demonstrating that this kind of fraud can happen anywhere, anytime.

During the mid-1980s, by focusing on the management of the overall company, Katharine and her

Graham holds an award she received from the Center of Communication in 1987. Presenting her the award are former chair of RCA, Thornton F. Bradshaw (left), and chair of Berkshire Hathaway Incorporated, Warren E. Buffett.

executive team were eventually able to create an efficient, world-class organization. In December 1988, the Washington Post Company was named one of the nation's five best-managed companies by a monthly business magazine, and a few years later, Katharine Graham received *Fortune* magazine's Business Hall of Fame award. After so many years of struggle and insecurity, things were going relatively smoothly for the company and its tireless head honcho.

Now that she was no longer saddled with the day-to-day operations of the newspaper with Don installed as publisher, Kay undertook a great deal of traveling with friend and colleague Meg Greenfield, and veteran reporter Jim Hoagland. "We logged tens of thousands of miles over the years traveling to South Africa, the Philippines, China, Korea, Japan, India, and countries throughout the Middle East and South America. Although Don Graham was the publisher of the *Post* and editorially responsible for the paper, with his encouragement I stayed involved in ways that never interfered with his authority. These trips were one way." During these journeys, the traveling team held interviews with heads of state such as Soviet leader Mikhail Gorbachev, Egyptian president Anwar Sadat, and Libyan leader Muammar Qaddafi. Especially in certain conservative, patriarchal Middle Eastern countries such as Saudi Arabia, Graham and Greenfield had to be very careful about how they dressed and behaved: the political leaders in such places were not accustomed to receiving important guests who happened to be female.

In the early 1990s, not too long after her 70th birthday, Graham finally decided to retire from the *Post*. The company was in great shape, and she still felt full of energy and ideas, but she was beginning to slow down. She wanted to devote her time to certain volunteer activities and, indeed, became very active in trying to improve educational and cultural opportunities for poor children of Washington, D.C. At this point she decided to write a memoir of her life. She explained her decision:

> Why dare to write a book? What makes any of us think that someone else would be interested in stories from our own past? For me, there was a mixture of motives. I had been thinking about my parents [both had died decades earlier], who, with their drive, discipline, eccentricity, and wealth, might be of interest even to nonfamily people. Also, I felt that Phil's story had not been told. . . . Partly, I wanted to look at my own life, because my personal history contains elements that were both unexpected and unrepeatable.

A natural journalist, Katharine was not satisfied with relying merely on her own memory of events but wanted to get as full and complete a picture as possible.

Graham delivers a speech standing beside a caricature of herself at a ceremony for the Reporters Committee for Freedom of the Press in May 2001, where she received a lifetime achievement award from the organization.

Over the course of several years, she and her researcher, Evelyn Small, conducted more than 250 interviews with individuals from Kay's childhood to those who knew her at the *Post*. The resulting book, called *Personal History*, was published in 1997. It became a number one best-seller and received great critical acclaim, winning the Pulitzer Prize for biography that year.

Asked by an interviewer how she felt about that achievement, Graham was not embarrassed to gush. "It is a thrill, you can't imagine. I never thought that anybody would read the book. When a lot of people read the book and then it got the prize, I just thought I had died and gone to heaven."

Humble yet exceedingly candid, filled with anecdotes both humorous and painful, and marked with the kind of observations and insights that will serve to instruct and inspire many new generations of women leaders to come, *Personal History* is a fitting capstone to a remarkable life.

Of course, Katharine did not feel that her public life ended with her memoir. In the years following the success of her book, she maintained her position on boards and committees such as the American Academy of Arts and Sciences and the National Campaign to Reduce Teenage Pregnancy. At the age of 84, Graham was still attending business conferences and delivering speeches.

Then in July 2001, at a conference for media executives in Sun Valley, Idaho, Graham fell on a sidewalk and suffered major head injuries. After spending a few days at a hospital in Boise, Graham died on July 17 of a brain hemorrhage, with her son Donald and other family members close by. The following week, a funeral service was held for her at the Washington National Cathedral in her hometown of Washington, D.C.

In her 84 years, Katharine Graham achieved more than most people aspire to—much of that success came in the second half of her life and after great tragedy. Her public achievements—the *Post* and its publishing company—are really just a piece of her personal legacy.

CHRONOLOGY

1917   Katharine "Kay" Meyer is born to Agnes Ernst Meyer and Eugene Meyer on June 16 in Mount Kisco, New York

1933   Eugene Meyer purchases the near-bankrupt *Washington Post*

1934   Katharine graduates from high school and enters Vassar; she later transfers to the University of Chicago

1938   Graduates from the University of Chicago and moves to San Francisco, where she works as a labor reporter at the *San Francisco News*

1939   Returns to Washington, D.C., to work for the *Post*

1940   Marries Phil Graham and moves into a house near Georgetown, in Washington, D.C.

1941   Phil enlists as an intelligence officer in the U.S. Army

1943   Graham gives birth to a daughter, Elizabeth "Lally" Graham

1945   Gives birth to another child, Donald; Phil is discharged from the armed forces after the war ends and goes to work for Eugene Meyer

1946   Eugene Meyer steps down and Phil Graham, just 31 years old, takes over as publisher of the *Post*

1948   Katharine gives birth to William

1951   Gives birth to Stephen, her last child; Eugene and Agnes transfer most of the controlling stock of the Washington Post Company to Katharine and Phil

1957   After several years of difficulties and triumphs at the *Post* and in his political endeavors, Phil goes through his first major, suicidal depression

1963   After a forced stint in a mental hospital, Phil returns to their country home and commits suicide; Graham soon takes over as publisher of the *Post*

1970   Women and minorities begin filing discrimination suits against the *Post*

1971   Graham decides to publish the Pentagon Papers

1972   The Watergate scandal is reported by *Post* journalists Bob Woodward and Carl Bernstein

1975   Workers strike against the *Post*

1979   Graham's son Don is named publisher of the *Post*; Graham retains her job as chairman and CEO of the Washington Post Company, now a half-billion dollar organization

1981   A fabricated front-page story written by Janet Cooke embarrasses the *Post*

1987   Graham turns 70 and retires

1988   The Washington Post Company is recognized for the first time as one of the best-managed organizations in the country

1997   Graham wins a Pulitzer Prize for *Personal History*, a memoir of her life

2001   Dies on July 17 after suffering head injuries during a fall

FURTHER READING

Bernstein, Carl, and Bob Woodward. *All the President's Men*. New York: Touchstone, 1994.

Bradlee, Ben. *A Good Life: Newspapering and Other Adventures*. New York: Touchstone, 1995.

Davis, Deborah. *Katharine the Great: Katharine Graham and Her Washington Post Empire*. New York: Sheridan Square Press, 1991.

Felsenthal, Carol. *Power, Privilege and the Post: The Katharine Graham Story*. New York: Seven Stories Press, 1999.

Graham, Katharine. *Personal History*. New York: Alfred A. Knopf, 1997

Greenfield, Meg, Katharine Graham, and Michael R. Beschloss. *Washington*. Washington, D.C.: Public Affairs, 2001.

Smith, Hedrick. *The Power Game: How Washington Works*. New York: Random House, 1988.

Woodward, Bob. *Shadow: Five Presidents and the Legacy of Watergate*. New York: Touchstone Books, 2000.

Websites

The Washington Post
   http://www.washingtonpost.com

Student Newspaper Network
   http://www.highwired.com

People of the Century–Katharine Graham Profile
   http://www.sacbee.com/news/projects/people_of_century/sci_biz/graham.html

INDEX

and passive role in
marriage, 39-40, 42,
48, 49, 52
and Pentagon Papers,
78-83, 102
personality of, 26-28,
39-40, 48, 52
and Phil as publisher
of *Washington Post*,
44-49, 62-63
and Phil's love affair,
14-15, 54-56, 57
and political issues,
28-30, 48, 66-68
as president and chair
of Washington Post
Company, 18
as president of American
Newspaper Publishers
Association, 106
as publisher of *Washington Post*, 17-18, 46,
61-73, 75-83, 85-91,
93-103, 105-106
and racial and women's
issues, 70-73
and relationship with
father, 18-19, 24, 29,
30, 48-49
and relationship with
mother, 23-24, 28,
29, 30, 48
and retirement from
Washington Post, 109
and social life, 54
as teenager, 26-28
and travel in later years,
108-109
and volunteer activities,
109, 111
and Watergate scandal, 102
Graham, Phil (husband)
and alcohol, 41-42, 48,
51-52, 56

as associate publisher of
Washington Post, 43
and attempted control
of Washington Post
Company, 57-58
children of, 13, 17, 40,
42, 43, 48, 56
and controlling stock of
Washington Post Company, 18-19, 48-49
and courtship with
Katharine, 34-35
and dominant role in
marriage, 39-40, 48,
49, 52
family of, 38-39
and first encounter with
Katharine, 33-34
and institutionalization,
15-16, 57, 59
as intelligence officer in
U.S. Army, 40-42
as lawyer, 34, 39
and love affair, 14-15,
54-56, 57
and manic depression,
14-17, 34, 48, 51-59,
62-63
and marriage, 37-38
and political issues, 53
as publisher of *Washington
Post*, 13, 15, 19, 43-49,
62-63
and relationship with
Phil, 34, 37, 43
and suicide, 15-17, 59
Graham, Stephen (Stevie)
(son), 17, 48
Graham, William (Bill)
(son), 17, 48
Great Depression, 24, 28
Greenfield, Meg
and strike against
Washington Post, 96

and travel with
Katharine, 108, 109
and Watergate scandal, 89

Hoagland, Jim, 108
Hoover, Herbert, 24
House Committee on
Un-American Activities
(HUAC), 46-48

Johnson, Claudia "Lady
Bird," 66
Johnson, Lyndon B., 17,
53
and lack of support
from *Washington Post*,
66-68
and Vietnam War, 76,
78, 81
Jones, Casey, 39

Kennedy, Jackie, 54
Kennedy, John F., 53
assassination of, 66
and relationship with
the Grahams, 17, 54,
56, 59
Kenney, George, 42

Lippman, Walter, 45, 64

McCarthy, Joseph, 46-48,
75
McGovern, George, 89
Madeira high school, 26, 27
Meagher, Mark, 96-97,
100, 102
Meyer, Agnes Ernst
(mother), 21-24, 28
as journalist, 22, 29, 48
and mental illness, 32-33
and relationship with
Katharine, 23-24, 28,
29, 30, 48

INDEX

and transfer of control-
ling stock to Phil,
18-19
and Vietnam War, 72,
77-83
and Watergate scandal,
85-91, 102, 107
and World War II, 72
See also Bradlee, Bill
Washington Post Company
Katharine as president
and chair of, 18

as one of nation's five
best-managed compa-
nies, 108
Phil owning controlling
shares of, 18-19
and Phil's attempt at
full control of, 57-58
Washington Star, 44, 99
Watergate scandal, 85-91,
102, 107
Webb, Robin, 14-15, 54-
56, 57

Welby, Glen, 15-16
Wiggins, Russ, 45, 54
Women's National Press
Club, 39
Women's Wear Daily, 70
Woodward, Bob, 87-88,
107
World Bank, 43
World War II, 30, 32, 38,
40, 42, 72

PICTURE CREDITS ═══════

Sandy Asirvatham, a graduate of Columbia University with a B.A. in philosophy and economics and a M.F.A. in writing, is a journalist, creative writer, and aspiring musician living in Baltimore. As a professional writer for more than 10 years, she has written extensively about business, government, and the arts for magazines and newspapers. Her other books for Chelsea House include a history of the police in America and an examination of the late 17th-century Salem witch trials.

Matina S. Horner was president of Radcliffe College and associate professor of psychology and social relations at Harvard University. She is best known for her studies of women's motivation, achievement, and personality development. Dr. Horner has served on several national boards and advisory councils, including those of the National Science Foundation, Time Inc., and the Women's Research and Education Institute. She earned her B.A. from Bryn Mawr College and her Ph.D. from the University of Michigan, and holds honorary degrees from many colleges and universities, including Mount Holyoke, Smith, Tufts, and the University of Pennsylvania.